WOMEN'S ANGER MANAGEMENT WORKBOOK

A MINDFUL GUIDE TO DE-ESCALATE EXPLOSIVE
EMOTIONS & OVERCOME NEGATIVE THINKING

LITTLE VICTORIES

© **Copyright Little Victories 2022 - All rights reserved.**

The content contained within this book may not be reproduced, duplicated, or transmitted without direct written permission from the author or the publisher.

Under no circumstances will any blame or legal responsibility be held against the publisher, or author, for any damages, reparation, or monetary loss due to the information contained within this book, either directly or indirectly.

Legal Notice:

This book is copyright protected. It is only for personal use. You cannot amend, distribute, sell, use, quote or paraphrase any part, or the content within this book, without the consent of the author or publisher.

Disclaimer Notice:

Please note the information contained within this document is for educational and entertainment purposes only. All effort has been executed to present accurate, up to date, reliable, complete information. No warranties of any kind are declared or implied. Readers acknowledge that the author is not engaged in the rendering of legal, financial, medical, or professional advice. The content within this book has been derived from various sources. Please consult a licensed professional before attempting any techniques outlined in this book.

By reading this document, the reader agrees that under no circumstances is the author responsible for any losses, direct or indirect, that are incurred as a result of the use of the information contained within this document, including, but not limited to, errors, omissions, or inaccuracies.

JUST FOR YOU!

A FREE GIFT *for our readers!*
This Rapid Relaxation Guide is a popular CBT treatment to relax, relieve stress and tension, anywhere at any time,
in **seconds**! Scan the QR code below!

CONTENTS

Introduction — 7

1. ARE WE BORN ANGRY? — 17
   Act Like a Lady — 17
   Anger Defined — 22
   Different Stages of Anger — 28
   Why Am I So Angry? — 33
   Empower Yourself With Self-Discovery — 37

2. ANGER CHANNELED INTO SOMETHING POSITIVE — 41
   "Angry" Women and Society — 41
   Making Anger Productive — 46
   Empower Yourself With Self-Compassion — 51

3. KNOW YOUR TRIGGERS — 57
   "Triggered" Isn't Just a Buzzword — 58
   Common Anger Triggers — 63
   How to Identify Your Personal Triggers — 65
   Moving Past Your Triggers — 67
   Hormonal Imbalance as Triggers — 69
   Menopause as a Trigger — 72
   Empower Yourself With Self-Identification — 75

4. GET TO THE ROOT CAUSE — 79
   What Are Your Emotions Really Telling You? — 80
   Anger and Gender Inequalities — 86
   Letting Go of Past Hurt to Heal the Present — 89
   Empower Yourself With Self-Freedom — 92

5. SELF-CARE AND THE POWER OF MINDFULNESS — 95
The Importance of Self-Care — 95
The Importance of Mindfulness — 100
Empower Yourself With Self-Care and Mindfulness — 102

6. COMMUNICATE EFFECTIVELY — 111
Effective Communication — 112
Restorative Communication — 121
Empower Yourself With Self-Empathy — 124

7. USE CBT STRATEGIES — 127
What Is Cognitive Behavioral Therapy? — 127
CBT for Anger Management — 129
Empower Yourself With Self-Reflection — 135

Conclusion — 139
A Place to Grow — 147

References — 151

INTRODUCTION

Holding on to anger is like grasping a hot coal with the intent of throwing it at someone else; you are the one who gets burned.

— BUDDHA

Anger can take many different forms, and the presence of this emotion in women has been considered taboo for many years. However, you and I—as women and human beings—have little outbursts of anger or frustration every day. If not every day, it likely happens a couple of times during the week, or for some of us, even multiple times per day. What is this feeling? We all feel it develop as a vortex in our stomachs, or maybe in an uncertain spot in our chests, and it escalates to a sensation of extreme heat in our brains. At that point, our head feels heavy and busy, and all our facial muscles contract too because of the intensity. This is anger, and it is that one feeling that will, sooner or later, be expressed in some way, internally or externally, because it cannot be contained for long.

Consider for a moment, the following scenarios:

In the first scenario, you are a young woman who has spent the whole day studying for your coming exam. The subject is mathematics. It is hard, but it is so for everyone. Despite that, your classmates and teacher think it will be harder for you because you are a female. They ask themselves: *Why is she studying mathematics at university and not literature? Why is she even at university?* You know what they think of you because in class, during teamwork, they act avoidant with you. They do not ask for your opinion on the correctness of the equation. You feel annoyed, and you ask yourself why you feel treated differently from your other classmates. Once you go home, you read on the internet that, in 2016, less than a third of the population employed in scientific subjects were women (Catalyst, 2018). You also read that when women manage to start a career in scientific environments, they face higher rates of discriminations and experience episodes of sexual harassment in their workplace (Funk & Park, 2018). Then, you feel angry and ask yourself: What is the point of studying mathematics if the world will be so hostile to you?

In the second scenario, you are a mother of three kids. However, you have not always been a mother. You were a hard-working young woman before getting pregnant, and you thought that once married, you and your husband would have found a way to raise your children together so that no one would have to stop working. Unfortunately, that was not the case. You had to quit your job because taking care of children is hard work and a full-time commitment. It is all-encompassing; it requires love and dedication, and you could not keep up with the stress of both family responsibilities and work together. This is when you experience mixed feelings. You see your beautiful children grow more and more fond of you because of your constant presence and affection, but you also miss your career and the possibility of being relevant in a working environment. You feel relieved that your children are healthy but frustrated that you do not have time for yourself anymore. Then you read the news, and you realize that you are not the only one. You read that, in Seoul, more than 60% of women quit their job right after getting pregnant, and approximately 81% of women did so even before giving birth to their first child (이동민, 2019). That is when you feel rather angry, and you ask yourself why so many women in the world are forced to choose between their family and their career.

In the third scenario, you are still a mother, but this time, you are very grateful that your husband's job is good enough to support the whole family. This allows you to do what you love most, being a mother, and it enables you to spend a lot of time taking care of your son and build a significant relationship with him. However, being a mother is not an easy job and can be unforgiving. Throughout your son's growth, you have always materially helped him: You cooked for him, did his laundry, picked him up from school, and taught him how to do basically everything. You have constantly emotionally supported him, comforted him when he was crying ever since his very first months and years of life, encouraged him to nourish his passions, taught him to never give up in front of obstacles, and gave him advice when he was finding himself in difficult situations. In response to your caring behavior, your son has always been very fond of you and has regarded you as a cornerstone of his life. However, now that he is a teenager, he is starting to act more avoidant and indifferent towards you. He now seeks more space for himself and acts rude when you try to ask him personal questions like you used to do when he was younger.

Because of your intrusiveness, he tells you one day that he is going to sleep at a friend's house. But you call the friend's mother to make sure that your son is behaving correctly, and she tells you that your son is not there. You realize that he lied to you. If, when your son was acting standoffish with you, you were feeling frustrated, now you feel pure anger. You cannot understand why, after so many years of struggles to build a relationship of mutual trust, he now lies to you as if you were a bad mother or worse, a stranger.

These are clearly only a few examples of reasons why a woman might feel very angry. There are so many other reasons why we might feel frustrated, misunderstood, hurt, or betrayed. It could be a difficult or toxic relationship with our partner, being constantly exposed to situations of violence and rage, not being able to establish significant relationships with our children, feeling lonely, and the list goes on. One study, which has collected data over the course of 15 years to explain women's anger, found that such feelings are mostly caused by difficult interpersonal relationships (Thomas, 2005). More specifically, among a sample of 535 American women, two-thirds of them exhibited feelings of anger when finding themselves in circumstances of powerlessness. This included the strong desire to change a specific situation and the impossibility of doing so. The study further found that anger was triggered in that sample by situations of injustice—scenarios where women were victims of sexist behaviors or inconsiderate treatments. This included instances of being mistreated by a partner or by the boss at work. It also noted triggers caused by unfair situations where their sons or partners were lying to them. It is important to note, a great stressor which induced feelings of anger was found to be the element of responsibility from family members. Women in the study described how most of their angst was caused by all the pressure they were subject to and the absence of any help coming from family members. They would have to do all the house chores by themselves, reflecting a more general situation where a woman does not receive the support she needs and constantly only gives without ever receiving gratitude or recognition in return. An important contributor to anger in that sample was found to be the tendency to not express their feelings, to not speak out, and to keep everything inside. In fact, 91% of the women revealed that they would not discuss their concerns with their family members and that they would try to solve their own problems without asking for help.

While all the indicators point out that the development of anger mainly derives from adverse socio-political situations of injustice, we do not need to think that such scenarios are much different from our everyday life. We are all part of a big society, and most of the time, anger arises from our constant interactions with others. If your circle of interactions is limited to your partner, or, rather, it expands to a large family or a very busy working environment, we all experience the same neurochemical phenomenon that eventually leads us to feel what we know as anger.

But what is this feeling? Is it bad for us? And why is it so widely spread among the female population?

First, let us highlight that anger is a physiological reaction to an adverse external situation. If it exists and if our brain and our body produce it, there must be a reason. Anger, indeed, exists to warn us that something is not quite correct, that we are experiencing a situation of injustice and that we need to come up with a solution. It does not exist to be ignored or repressed. When, during the day, you experience a very upsetting event, you might react with an outburst of anger which leaves everyone shocked. I bet you have heard multiple times the phrase, "You are being dramatic," or "You are clearly overreacting." When the episode of anger is over, you then convince yourself that you were indeed being too dramatic and that your reaction was extreme. Then, you calm down and you think you will never have such a bad reaction again. But what you have done is just convince yourself that your reaction was *not normal* and that it was somehow extraneous from you. However, you must not ignore that what has caused that explosive reaction is still out there, ready to trigger your anger again. This is because the provocative factor has not yet been identified, correctly and rationally processed, and, most importantly, made inoffensive.

Anger management requires work and involves making yourself aware of what is causing it and how you are expressing it. Part of this work also includes understanding that your anger is not a bad or disruptive feeling and that it does not have to be suppressed. Anger management is not about learning how to stop feeling angry or how to stop expressing it but rather developing healthier forms of expelling it.

There will always be instances where we want to depend on our anger to help us feel strong in a helpless moment. That dependency can become a bad habit very quickly, and the only way to break it is to begin with small changes. By incorporating the techniques mentioned throughout this book, you can reconfigure how you approach triggering situations by recontextualizing and shifting your frame of mind. You picked up this book with a goal in mind, and while it is important to understand why you are embarking on this journey, remember that a goal without a change in your patterns is unsustainable. Your system must change to not only achieve your goal but also set up a healthy foundation to do so again in the future because we are always going to be works in progress. If you backslide or make a mistake, it is okay. You fortify your strength and character by picking this book up again whenever and if ever you need to read through it again.

This book is specifically tailored to all those women who, less or more frequently, experience feelings of rage and anger. It is meant to be a detailed and approachable guide to show you that violence and frustrations are not the only forms into which anger can transform, but rather that you can master a unique way of expressing your feelings in a much healthier manner. If you have spent hours fantasizing about an ideal life where you are in complete harmony with your family or surroundings, this book will allow you to allow that wish to come to fruition. By teaching you how to get to know your inner triggers, your feelings, and thought processes, this book will enable you to become a better version of yourself—a version you are entirely capable of becoming will just a little help.

1

ARE WE BORN ANGRY?

Do not let your anger lead to hatred, as you will hurt yourself more than you would the other.

— STEPHEN RICHARDS

ACT LIKE A LADY

According to the scientific survey we have consulted to gather some general information on why women tend to feel angry, we have learned that such feelings arise more often when a woman feels constricted in a situation of powerlessness and injustice (Thomas, 2005). But why do women seem to find themselves in those circumstances? Why does it happen so often, and is our society structured in a way in which those feelings are inevitable? According to Ellen Lois, who has written an article for the magazine *Career Girl Daily*, there are five etiquette behaviors that girls nowadays perpetuate without even being aware of it (Lois, 2016). These behaviors would be:

- the tendency to speak politely and avoid the use of jargon and swear words
- being loyal and trustworthy
- always being approachable and exhibiting a good attitude so that people will have a good impression of you
- always keeping the phone in their bag and avoiding being on the phone while in company
- always wearing outstanding clothes with the intention of impressing the crowd, but somehow also remaining chaste and demure

According to a study conducted by Alexandra Jane Allan (2008), interviewing girls of a single-sex private primary school in the south of Britain, the idea of having to embody the perfect figure of a lady is still very much strong, even emerging from such a young age. When conducting her study, she found that the girls were feeling obliged to develop the characteristics of being polite, girly, well-mannered, sexy, and respectable, typical of middle-class young women. Such ideas were encouraged by the schoolteachers: The young ladies fostered "lady-like" behaviors by sitting up straight at the lunch table, avoiding speaking with their mouths open, and not leaving the table until the lunch was over.

If we notice a strong embodiment of the concepts of femininity in primary school girls, what happens when women start a career and enter the professional world? According to Melanie Buddle (2006), women in mid-20th century British Columbia became entrepreneurs while still being careful to maintain their femininity. This is not a negative thing, certainly if a woman loves to dress in a certain way, it is right for her to do so while going to work. However, the point that the author makes in this article is a bit different. She says that women in British Columbia employ their feminine traits of respectability and devotion to family to demonstrate that they can be trustworthy and responsible in the working environment, too. But, most importantly, the author stresses how these women are still occupying positions above other women, only. They still choose to run businesses in the "feminine" field of clothing, cooking, and ruling girls' schools. The situation remained the same throughout the years 1920–1980.

Did anything change afterward? According to Lori Chandler (2015), it would be "unnatural" to bring and maintain feminine features of insecurity and kindness to the working environment. This is because, she explains, every workplace requires the so-called more masculine ideal of competition to grow and reach higher positions, and women, just like men, have this feature innate in themselves. Chandler says that being competitive and tough is natural and healthy not only for men, but for women as well. She looks at the matter in evolutionary terms: Women have always had to be competitive to win the partner they desire. These days, a competitive nature also enables women to fight for their dream job position in the workplace. Is she right? Well, sort of.

A study conducted at Durham University by Anne Campbell (2004), who examined the question of competition among women in evolutionary and biological terms, mentioned that the trait of competition is much less pronounced in women as compared to men. Campbell explains why, evolutionarily speaking, women tend to be less competitive than men. She does so in terms of physical differences and chances of survival. If women are found to be the major caregiver for their children, men's main role remains that of competing with other men to attract the female that will give them offspring and assure the survival of their genes. However, we are obviously not only the result of evolutionary accounts of survival. Moreover, current society does not exactly work in the mechanical terms described by evolutionary accounts. Women have extensively fought for their rights to representation, starting from the first half of the 19th century and continuing today. This initially was urged by women who were demanding the right to vote, but it soon extended to many different realms of political and social nature.

The resentment of misogyny has very old roots, having emerged in the Middle Age, but women did not structure into a revolutionary movement until the rise of feminism in the 19th century. In fact, in the 18th century, the question of femininity and "acting like a lady" was still at its peak. Specifically, in that period several feminine behavior etiquettes emerged, such as Florence Hartley's *The Ladies' Book of Etiquette, and Manual of Politeness* explaining how women were supposed to behave and dress at certain times of the day and during specific circumstances, as well as pointing out the duty of women to pursue a social career and invest their time in charity. However, times have changed, and as Lori Chandler (2015) points out, societal expectations of certain roles of women are unrealistic. It is not fair to expect that women will enter the working environment without exhibiting much competitiveness, as it is so when expecting that men will not express emotions and only ever exhibit masculine behaviors.

Lastly, when women are told to act like ladies, one must point out that many famous and successful historical figures did not properly embody the qualities of femininity as they are generally known. An example is Queen Eleanor of Aquitaine, the wife of King Henry II of England. She was calculative, competitive, independent, and authoritarian. Furthermore, think of Queen Marie Antoinette, the last Queen of France. Through her kingdom, she rebelled against the etiquette of a respectable ruler and a devoted and loyal wife. She exploited her position to live in glitz and splendor, was very controversial, and had many different lovers.

ANGER DEFINED

After having pointed out how situations of injustice, responsibility, and the feeling of powerlessness have been found to be the leading causes of the development of anger in women, we have also shown how women nowadays are still constrained into the roles of feminine ideals. Either in working environments or life in society, they are still bound to the condition of having to show off their best qualities *as women*, always, in every circumstance. If this social constraint is not the only reason for the development of anger in women, it could still be one leading cause.

Regardless of the main trigger for rage, we still need to address the physiological and psychological roots of this feeling so that we can properly understand its nature.

Anger, like any other phenomenon occurring in our bodies, is not a simple event. In fact, it is determined by many different elements manifesting on the physical level. First, it is an emotion, and like other emotions, it arises in a specific part of our brain called the amygdala. Anger is usually defined as a mental and physical response to a threatening stimulus, and it is highly triggered by frustration. Frustration is that emotion arising when someone is expecting to receive a reward, but that reward does not come. The amygdala plays a fundamental role in anger and is located in the middle part of the brain, wedged between the temporal lobes adjacent to the hippocampus, and it is responsible for many different phenomena. Among its roles, it is responsible for the regulation of decision-making (involving the emotional aspect of it, rather than the rational one controlled by the frontal cortex), memory processing, and, most importantly, the perception and regulation of emotions. If we want to understand the mechanics of anger, we first need to address the matter of reactive aggression. Reactive aggression is a phenomenon that occurs when a person is faced with unexpected frustrating situations, and, consequently, the person will directly attach the perceived source to such frustration.

As we mentioned earlier on, anger and aggression are not negative and detrimental bodily responses. Inversely, they have evolved in the human brain to support survival, and for this reason, they are very ancestral emotions: They are present in every mammalian species, not only humans, and they enable the proper defense from threatening stimuli. According to scientific literature (Blair, 2011), threatening situations can be perceived as either low or high. When a circumstance is perceived as discreet or not so dangerous but still suspicious, the bodily response in all mammals, including humans, would be to freeze in place. The animal or the individual, when they perceive a possibly dangerous situation, activates all five senses to identify the element of threat and respond accordingly. On the other hand, when the threat is perceived to be very high, it induces the perceiver to escape and find a way to get away from the threat. Here is where anger comes into play. Anger is a necessary bodily response that is induced when the threat is perceived to be extremely high and close but when escape is impossible. The animal or individual, in this case, would react with an outburst of reactive aggression, which would exponentially increase their chances of survival. In this way, anger plays the role of a body alarm, which warns us when to act in a certain way, to guarantee our survival and wellbeing.

If we consider, for one moment, what happens on a physical level, I am certain this description would ring a bell to anyone reading this book: When the feeling of anger is triggered, there are several physiological impulses that prepare the body for the reactive aggression.

First, as the sensation of being angry starts to develop, all the muscles of your body become very tense.

At the same time, you would start experiencing a very strong feeling of energy build-up, which does not end shortly after but would rather last several minutes. This energy accumulation is caused by the release of specific brain chemicals in response to external or hormonal stress. These chemicals are known as the neurotransmitter catecholamines, which are hormones produced by adrenal glands, and include dopamine, norepinephrine, and adrenaline.

After this phenomenon, a series of precipitating events take place. When you get angry, you might recall the instance of feeling your heartbeat accelerating, which means that your blood pressure is now elevated. Your face would turn red given the increase of blood flow going through your body. Your attention, as well, is subject to modifications: For those moments when all these physical changes are occurring, you cannot divert your thought and attention from the target of your anger outburst. Now, everything in your body is ready for you to fight the threat. If this scenario portrays a situation that could easily exit from the control of the person experiencing it, the amygdala does not work alone. As I briefly mentioned earlier, the prefrontal cortex can take the rational control of how to direct and exert this feeling. In fact, the relationship between the amygdala (causing all the bodily symptoms) and the prefrontal cortex (making rational judgments) is in perfect balance in healthy individuals, who are capable of tailoring anger towards its more effective function. Those individuals who have mastered the ability to control anger outbursts experience the canonical and progressive diminution of physiological arousal once the prefrontal cortex has been successfully recruited.

In this phase, all our muscles would progressively relax, as we start to rationally realize that the threat we had identified as dangerous is no longer a reason for concern. However, to reach our resting state after an episode of anger is not an immediate and straightforward action—this book will walk you through how to get there. Inversely, given that the state of adrenaline is not immediately calmed, this will lower our anger threshold, making it easier for us to get angry the next time. A threshold in physiology is the minimum intensity—or voltage—that a cell needs to reach in order for the given action to be initiated. Think of it as a domino effect: The threshold for a little glass marble sitting on a perfectly straight surface is that tiny push to make it start rolling and hitting the following object. This tiny push needs to be strong enough, in proportion with the weight and size of the ball, so that it starts rolling and reaches the closest object. In the case of anger, it works slightly differently. The more often an anger outburst is caused without control, the more often the biological system will adapt to the physiological changes and will produce more and more severe bodily reactions. This is because the "anger cells" will progressively need less significant threats to be triggered. In a few words, the more often you get uncontrollably angry, the more difficult it will be for you to control the future rage attacks you will have, which in turn will be more intense. If you do not learn how to manage your anger and bodily responses, you will just be more susceptible, irritable, and less capable of controlling yourself in front of everyday life challenges.

DIFFERENT STAGES OF ANGER

Triggers

Since we have given an overview of the physiological changes that take place in your body during an anger outburst, let us now break down each element of an anger attack and point out its main features. Anger triggers can metaphorically be compared to a flower seed. They are hidden and not immediately accessible to the sight but are so important in determining the quality of the flower; they also need to be watered and taken care of. To give a definition, a *trigger* is a sensitive element present in everyone's life—although there is usually more than one in each person—which can get activated by certain circumstances and people.

Injustice, relationship fights, disappointment, and disrespect form the first cluster of triggers identified to be most common among people. I have isolated this first group because, if you remember, these are exactly the reasons for which women in the study by Thomas (2005) were found to develop feelings of anger. These elements of discord are common to everybody. Injustice appears to be the first and most severe trigger of anger for everyone. This is because injustice can be anywhere, regardless of your social, political, and economical background. Injustice can be a promotion at work given to someone you feel did not deserve it as much as you. It can also involve being wrongly accused or mistreated solely based on your physical appearance: Women wearing short dresses, for example, are much more likely to be sexually harassed than women wearing long coats and clothes that generally hide their body shapes.

One of the most socially triggering phenomena experienced by women is workplace sexual harassment (SH). Research on this topic has been conducted for over 40 years, and this attention started to gain traction in the early 1970s. Due to the amount of investigation carried on, we now know that SH occurs with a frequency of 40–75% of American women experiencing it (McDonald, 2012). Importantly, however, the rate of SH detected when asking participants based on the legal definition of this phenomenon if they have experienced it or not is much lower as compared to when SH is tested psychologically (using psychometric scales where SH is not directly addressed). This means that there might be issues with the legal definitions of SH, urging a redefinition of them to be more inclusive and allowing women to properly address this dangerous phenomenon.

These sorts of social injustices can raise a great deal of discontent which causes anger and rage from the victim groups. Expressions of such anger can be public protests and revolts. It follows that the feeling of disappointment found to be among the most frequent triggers for anger, in general, corresponds to the element of powerlessness—identified by Thomas (2005) experienced by women. According to Vassar (2011) other very common triggers in the general population are physical threats, abusive language, and violation of personal spaces. Understanding your triggers, which can be among the ones identified or different and personal ones, is the key to success in anger management. The identification of individual and unique triggers depends on life experiences. Re-living a situation that in the past made you very angry can cause future rage episodes. The problem with most individuals is that they are not aware of their triggers and need professional consultancy to identify and take control of them.

The Escalation Cycle

What we have described on a physiological level is commonly known as the Aggression Cycle. Let us give a closer look at the specific phases of this cycle. The escalation, which we have already talked about, concerns all those triggering events that prepare your body to deal with a proper anger attack. When discussing this phase, it is important to point out that an escalation is not necessarily and immediately caused by one single event. Instead, an escalation can be triggered over the long run.

Imagine the situation where you are experiencing a very stressful and tough week. During the day, you collect different anger cues, which are little annoying events that, when accumulated, will eventually cause an anger explosion. This is caused when all the anger cues you are unconsciously detecting are consciously ignored. You are unaware of them, but your system knows that they are occurring. It is the moment when you cannot take it anymore; you have accumulated so much stress, and it feels to you as if everything happening around you just annoys you and irritates you more. This feeling of anger build-up is the most important to be detected on time because it prevents you from degenerating and reaching the explosion phase. If it goes undetected, that is when we reach the *crisis phase*: You are forced to choose how to react to the perceived danger. It reflects the commonly known fight or flight response, and your brain might decide to overtly react, by shouting, raising your voice, or even throwing things and trying to harm the person who is upsetting you. On the other hand, your brain might decide to "fly" and make you react by internalizing your anger or maybe leaving the place and bursting out in tears.

Whatever your reaction has been, your body will, sooner or later, cool down. This is called the *recovery phase*, where you are brought to a pre-anger state. However, this can last several hours or days, and, here, you are more susceptible to anger triggers. You can certainly picture the image of you being upset for several hours after an anger attack, but you know you have control of your surroundings, and this feeling is more like annoyance rather than rage. Here, though, the slightest trigger could make you explode again, so you need to take some time by yourself, or surround yourself with positive elements.

Despite you having calmed down and feeling that your anger episode belongs to the past, every action you take has consequences for your immediate future. The so-called *post-explosion phase* consists of all those consequences that an anger explosion has on a single individual. These can be experiencing feelings of shame and guilt for the previous event, but even more contingent consequences vary depending on the severity of the anger outburst—such as losing your job, your close relationships with your partners or friends, or even going to jail. You cannot delete what happened just by forgetting it because it will come back even stronger, following this exact cycle pattern. It is important for you to learn how to recognize the different phases and act upon them before they are fatally initiated.

WHY AM I SO ANGRY?

The expression of rage attacks does not only have detrimental effects in your immediate present. Conversely, it can significantly impair different aspects of your life, and it might do so in a way that is uncontrollable. Anger can disrupt fundamental cognitive abilities that all healthy individuals have—decision-making and judgment. Litvak and colleagues (2010) explain how anger can be a very dangerous feeling when people experience it frequently but must fulfill their social duties at the same time. They point out that anger narrows your attention, making it impossible to mentally multitask and makes your brain only focus on your anger cues. This can impair your work performance and you will miss out on important details in your immediate surroundings. This also impairs your ability to make decisions: Every decision you make will be subtly dictated by anger and will not reflect your ability to discriminate between what is good and what is wrong. They also say that anger affects a wide range of personality traits, making the angry person very punitive in their judgments, and narrowing other's perceptions of them as authoritarian, threatening, and dominant. It can also affect your everyday relationships, as people will be less likely to reach out to you when they need emotional support or any kind of help.

Uncontrolled anger also has several detrimental consequences on your health. Excessive anger outbursts and even the accumulation of repressed anger is greatly associated with the weakening of your immune system. A study conducted by Romero-Martínez and colleagues (2016), testing the effect of recalling an event where anger was experienced, found that the sampled group were expressing a lowering of antibody immunoglobulin A levels, lasting six hours. Another side effect that anger can have on your health is increasing the likelihood of developing respiratory problems. According to Zubzansky (2006) who conducted a study on a large number of individuals scoring high on the hostility scale, people suffering from anger management issues tend to have significantly lower lung capacity. Anger also increases your chances of developing severe cardiovascular events, such as myocardial infarction (heart attack), acute coronary syndrome (a condition that causes reduced blood reaching the heart), and hemorrhagic stroke (Mostofsky and colleagues, 2014).

Along with such disruptive physical disturbances that can be caused by excessive anger, there are some psychological issues to be considered as well. We will briefly mention anxiety and depression because they can be considered as both consequences and causes of anger, exhibiting high chances of comorbidity (the simultaneous presence of two or more diseases). First, despite irritability not being listed among possible comorbidities of depression, psychiatrist Dr. Maurizio Fava says that it can be, especially for the children and adolescent age groups (Greenfieldboyce, 2019). He further explains that the phenomenon of anger in depressed individuals can be exhibited as panic attacks or bipolar disorder events. He suggests that depression can follow an anger attack in the form of remorse: You might indeed experience a calming down period where you feel completely alienated from reality, and you are overwhelmed with feelings of sadness and self-reproach for your behavior during the rage episode. During his clinical experience with patients, he has also diagnosed individuals taking antidepressants as having anger attacks. His opinion is also backed up by studies showing a straightforward link between depression and anger. An investigation conducted by Judd and colleagues (2013) found that symptoms of irritability were present in more than half of their sample group affected by MDE (major depressive episodes). The presence of such symptoms of anger was found to exacerbate the depression, making it more severe and longer lasting. The comorbidity of these two conditions also caused reduced life satisfaction and expectancy, as well as reduced anger control. We can see then how both issues of anger and depression worsened each other, forming a very dangerous cycle for those who experience them.

According to scientific research, anger can also cause severe anxiety attacks. Symptoms of internalized anger (which is the anger that you don't express but keep within you for days and days) make anxiety symptoms progressively worse (Deschênes and colleagues, 2012). You might empathize with these findings. Just think for a moment of your worst weeks when you were triggered by so many annoying events that were making you angrier and angrier. But your life had to go on. You had to keep up with the pace of it—maybe bringing your kids to school, doing the house chores, or surviving a very long day at the office. Do you remember that weight in your chest and stomach? You were probably feeling anxious that those cues that were making you so irritable would not stop. However, everyone is different, and the conditions that go hand in hand with irritability certainly do not stop there.

The understanding of the emotion of anger is not very easy and straightforward, given that multiple factors contribute to its complexity. There are physiological, as well as evolutionary and cultural elements involved, reasons for which a full comprehension of it is occurring right now through empirical research and field study. Overall, you should not feel discouraged if you cannot get to the bottom of where your anger comes from. Always remember that you can reach out to professional help at any time, being that anger is such a complex and multifaceted emotion. It is enough for you to have understood where the feeling of anger comes from and to be strong and motivated enough to change it. In the following chapters, you will be faced directly with your triggers and root causes and will go through a journey specifically tailored to the understanding of your innermost self. You will also learn how to appreciate this feeling, give a name to it, and modify its disruptive features.

EMPOWER YOURSELF WITH SELF-DISCOVERY

As you might have understood from this first chapter, when it comes to anger issues, understanding how each one of us expresses it is key to the success in managing it. The following are three exercises that will ideally make you more aware of your anger expressions. I suggest you do these exercises again every time that you feel you are accumulating irritability (during a tough week or period) or when you feel yourself approaching the escalation phase.

Exercise: Getting to Know My Anger

This exercise has the aim of introducing you to your feelings of anger, being able to pinpoint them, and learning how to recognize them in the future. As discussed, naming your anger has the power of giving you control over it. If you manage to associate a name or label to a feeling you are experiencing, it makes you more likely to isolate it, recognize it, and be able to positively act upon it.

This exercise will train you to differentiate between the feelings you felt at the moment of the event from the ones you are feeling now that you are only remembering it. To do so, you will need to look at the situation through the eyes of a spectator. Try to rephrase the whole situation in your head using the third person singular and refer to yourself as if you were someone else. In the scene, the real you is sitting on a bench and only witnessing the event. Allow yourself to judge the episode, by giving your opinion and how you felt watching it. Write on a piece of paper how you feel now while remembering the episode from an external point of view. Do you maybe feel worried, annoyed, or empathetic? You might realize that these feelings are very different from the ones you felt in the moment of the heated event. You are now able to rationally give advice to your old self concerning other ways to deal with the situation.

This exercise altogether will enable you to recognize your feelings before they overwhelm you and become indiscernible—before they take the form of a confused and chaotic anger outburst. You should also be able to apply these rational suggestions to new situations because you are able to detect them and break them down prior to any uncontrollable escalation of emotion.

2

ANGER CHANNELED INTO SOMETHING POSITIVE

There is nothing wrong with anger, provided you use it constructively.

— WAYNE DYER

"ANGRY" WOMEN AND SOCIETY

The state of our current society imposes a double standard when it comes to expressing feelings of rage. Using the words of writer and activist Denise Dudley on women: "We are considered to be difficult when we get angry, whereas men are perceived to be tough and powerful" (Fottrell, 2019). This preconception towards women as being overtly emotional by nature causes a huge deal of consequences that make the figure of the woman even more overlooked and disregarded. If society continues to explain women's moments of anger as a mere expression of their emotional nature, then any form of verbal protest will continue to be deemed as irrelevant and unimportant. Furthermore, if women keep being restricted by the standard of "acting like a lady," they will always be expected to act cool and maintain their calm even during events of extreme injustice.

But it is exactly these perceptions of unfairness, powerlessness, and stereotyping that cause women to feel so much anger. Here, we are confronted with a vicious cycle. We cannot conform to societal standards because these have been proven to cause serious harm to our mental health, making us develop unhealthy mechanisms of rage and fury, which in turn we are not free to express. After all, we would only be labeled as emotional by nature. What is the solution then? We need to stress that we are not learning how to manage our anger to conform to societal standards; we are learning to do so to ameliorate our mental health, disclose anger's benefits and purposes, and ensure a healthier mutual relationship with people in our society. Conversation is always the key to success, both for women and men.

When thinking about the whole spectrum of emotions, we tend to label happiness, amusement, admiration, and surprise as positive feelings. But we tend to consider anger, shame, fear, and jealousy as negative. Why so? Why do we think of anger as a purely negative emotion? It should be a positive emotion, something without which we would not be so good at protecting ourselves from external threats. According to Soraya Chemaly (2018), another writer and activist, this has very much to do, once again, with gender roles! In her article, she describes an event that occurred during her childhood that provided a perfect example to prove her point. One day she witnessed her mother smashing all the plates of her precious wedding china from the kitchen window. The woman, according to Chemaly's description, had always been very quiet and gentle, and she kept such temperament even during such an outburst of silent anger. What was extremely striking for the writer, a girl of 15 years at the time of the episode, was that her mother chose to destroy specifically those plates, which constituted the most important and precious gift of her wedding. They were undoubtedly symbols of marital union and family approval and were cherished. Her mother kept them as relics, without ever using them, until that very day when she destroyed them one by one. Soraya thought that her mother did not see her watching, because right after this outstanding event, her mother casually went to ask her how her day at school had been, without expressing the slightest sign of anger or distress.

She comments on this episode in light of how our society differentiates how women express anger versus how men express anger. Imagine the scenario where a white businessman raises his voice to make his opinion more valuable in a given context: His colleagues would consider him with respect, to be authoritarian, and a born leader. What if a woman does the same? Chances are she will be labeled as frustrated, hysterical, and bossy. In Chemaly's article, she portrays exactly the picture of a society that shuts down women's voices by pointing fingers at them when they attempt to express angry emotions. That is why her mother was smashing plates a moment before and then casually having a cheerful conversation with her a moment after. Soraya, in another article, stresses how the cry of a woman usually makes people be more tender with them (Williams, 2018). If a woman goes to the police to report a theft or abuse, she is more likely to be heard and supported if she begins to cry. But she also points out that such a cry highlights a state of desperation and stress build-up. It is the exacerbation of anger, which, if repressed, might then take the form of bitter tears.

But why do women need to reach such a state of desperation to obtain what men simply get by raising their voice a bit too much?

This concept of angry women being considered hysterical is not new to current society but traces as far back as ancient Greece. That is where the term "hysteria" was first used by Plato and Hippocrates to describe the proneness of women to develop such conditions of irritability, due to the fact they had a womb. Many centuries later, in the 18th and 19th centuries, scientists and practitioners of that time started to employ the term "hysteria" to describe a mainly female condition that would later be broken down into post-traumatic stress disorder, depression, or anxiety (with no distinction of gender). Because hysteria was thought to mainly affect women due to their "natural irritable temperament," the cures developed to treat this condition were mainly reserved for women. In the few cases where a man would be found to be affected by hysteria, the most canonical cure imparted in the 19th century was just exercising outdoors: walking, running in the parks, and generally ignoring it, because it was not regarded as severe or dangerous to men. On the other hand, female hysteria was regarded as very problematic, and all sorts of treatments were invented. One of these treatments was the "rest cure" for which women were forced to stay in bed for long periods of time, thinking that would heal their condition. It clearly did not.

There is a very interesting account of this treatment prescribed to a woman. Charlotte Perkins Gilman wrote the book *The Yellow Wallpaper* describing the psychological distress she experienced during this "cure." The author talks about her confinement to a lonely room of a summer mansion, where she was basically imprisoned by her husband and her physician to treat her symptoms of hysteria. The decline of her mental health is shown through her gradual cognitive decline exhibited in the writing. As she spends day after day locked in the room she starts focusing on the wallpaper and starts seeing things that do not exist. This novel is nowadays considered an example of gothic literature, because of its redundant theme of powerlessness and mental violence. It is interesting to think that two centuries later, the women of Thomas' 2005 study said that one of the leading causes for their feelings of anger is powerlessness itself.

MAKING ANGER PRODUCTIVE

The observation in an earlier section of the physiological changes our bodies go through when experiencing an anger outburst taught us that anger is not always a bad feeling. It evolved to assist us when we are confronted with a dangerous situation. Subsequently, what we need to do is to learn how to use this evolutionary tool for the best and most productive purpose.

I would like to share the content of a tweet from someone who expressed her therapist's words about anger. The therapist said that anger is a feeling that knows all the abuses and mistreatments you were subject to, without you even being aware of them. It is an unconscious emotion that accumulates your frustrations and resentments to protect you from their repercussions. For this reason, their therapist says, anger is that part of you that loves you (Mahmoud, 2020). So, how do we properly let anger love us?

In addition to all the physical and psychological problems that anger can lead us to, as discussed above, an excessive amount of anger suppressed can also make us overtly aggressive and violent. First, anger itself has a biasing element: People who have anger management issues will tend to blame others and fail to be objective in the situation. This element makes the investigation of reasons for anger very hard to conduct, because individuals may not give rational explanations for their feelings. This phenomenon is commonly known as "hostile attribution bias," and refers to the instance where a very angry person will tend to see the external environment as hostile and unwelcoming, thus excusing their own behavior as a way to protect themselves from such hostility (Novaco, 2011). Think of those days when your stress reached its limit, you could not take any more, and you saw all your surroundings as hostile and the people around you as enemies. This has happened to all of us, and the roots of such phenomena trace back to the ancient era of Stoic philosophers, such as Seneca and Galen. They as well were discussing the topics of anger and how to channel it into positive emotions. They were referring to self-discipline. The existence of a hostile attribution bias in angry people will lead them to think in a way that will reinforce their anger schemas, deeply ingrained emotional patterns that repeat throughout our lives, sabotaging our attempts to reach our potential for mental well-being. It is fascinating to realize that philosophers belonging to the 1st and 2nd centuries—before Christ—were talking about the same concepts we currently find prevalent in our society, further demonstrating how we are all the products of years and years of societal behaviors and human history.

Second, a long-term benefit of anger could be its potential of pushing you to change things in your life. If you have managed to identify elements that calm you down, another activity you should invest your time with is identifying the elements that negatively affect your life. This is a very hard task to do, especially if you are not a person who is used to drastic changes. It can also be difficult because you would need to be able to rationally identify elements in your life that you have probably internalized and integrated as part of yourself. Do not worry, you are not alone in this; some people require years and years of professional help and therapy to be able to get rid of toxic elements in their life or in their subconscious. So, if you feel like there is nothing wrong with your life but keep on experiencing anger outbursts toward the same situation or person, it could be a good idea to seek professional help. A therapist can guide you through techniques that bring negative elements in your life to the surface; these could be simple aspects to fix but could also correspond to darker components buried deep down inside of you.

Let us consider some examples. A potential toxic component in your life could be a dysfunctional relationship with your partner, but perhaps you two have been dating for so long (and have children together) that you don't remember your life without them. Having a completely synchronous life is not a bad thing at all, but romantic relationships need to be healthy and balanced, which is not an easy goal to achieve. Identifying the key features of your relationships that negatively affect you will help you change how you deal with these issues and might also enable you to identify causes of anger.

Another important element of a healthy life is to set up your boundaries and make sure that your close ones always respect them. You might be aware of the things that make you happy, such as meeting your friends, sunbathing, reading a book, or whatever feels good for you. However, you might have not deeply identified and analyzed the elements that are truly important to you, those on which your entire happiness and peace of mind depend. It is important for you to do multiple lists this time. First, you should think of all the elements and activities that make you feel happy and peaceful. Among these, you should then pick the ones which are entirely necessary to you. This will help you set your boundaries.

Let us imagine the following scenario: It is a sunny day, and you and your partner are discussing how to spend your day off from work together. Your suggestion would be to go to the beach and sunbathe because you love the sea, and you have been waiting for this day for the entire week. Your partner, however, tells you that the exposure to the sun makes him feel dizzy and that, generally, he is not a big lover of the beach. He suggests instead to go have lunch at a nice restaurant.

Now here, what is your priority? You might choose to accommodate your partner because that would be your only day off together and because you appreciate their invitation to the restaurant. You realize that your partner is trying to make up for the fact that they don't share your passion for the beach by taking you on a nice date. But what happens when you are confronted with another circumstance?

Picture that scenario where every time that you plan to go out with your friends, your partner is making up excuses to prevent you from going. Maybe one day they are complaining about you leaving them alone, and another day they propose something more exciting. You notice this pattern, and you instantly feel the need to set up your boundaries. How you do this is very important. If you react with anger, you might only feed his insecurities and make him feel worse. But, instead, if you confront the situation with a healthy conversation, you might avoid developing feelings of resentment. You might also understand your partner's point of view and gain a deeper understanding of their mental health.

EMPOWER YOURSELF WITH SELF-COMPASSION

Exercise 1: Exploring My Anger

This first exercise will focus on getting to know your personal feeling of anger and break it down into smaller parts. As we said earlier, the first step is to isolate a feeling, so give it a name. Forming a schema in your brain about emotion is not as easy as doing so for concrete objects. When, as a child, you learn what a chair is and how it looks, you will be able to recognize it throughout the rest of your life, even if it will have a different color, shape, and size. When it comes to identifying the key features that define an emotion, the situation is more complex. This can be due to a variety of reasons. For example, women have been taught to suppress strong emotions, and thus the specific indicators might be hidden from our conscious perception. We only know that we have a wide vocabulary of terms to describe feelings, but we are perhaps not entirely sure which term works better for ourselves.

To make the identification job a little bit easier, try to take a piece of paper and write down the words that come up in your head when you think of the reasons that made you angry on a specific occasion. These can be "frustration," "irritation," "annoyance," "disappointment," or any word that would reflect your state of mind during that time. Then, based on the words you have selected, try to insert them inside phrases that would describe the situation when you felt angry. This might help you to consolidate them and recognize those feelings more quickly the next time you will experience them. Next, try to identify other terms that could describe other feelings that you felt at that time: Perhaps as well as being "disappointed," you were also "sad" and "hurt." Next, you might want to go back in time and think about how you reacted following your anger escalation and also think of the consequences your anger had. Lastly, you are left with considering, based on your conclusions, how differently you could have behaved.

Think about whether a different reaction could have changed the aftermath of your fight and led to different consequences.

Exercise 2: My Rainbow of Emotions

This exercise is aimed at reminding you how complex of a human you are and how many emotions are in your rainbow. Initial research on human emotions revealed the existence of only six of them: anger, fear, disgust, happiness, sadness, and surprise. However, as more research has been done on our complexities, this array significantly increased. According to a recent study conducted at Berkeley University by Cowen and Keltner (2017), humans experience as many as 27 different emotional states. Interestingly, emotions like anger and happiness were not on the list, which instead included feelings such as admiration, empathetic pain, and sexual desire. The 27 emotions can add together to form more involved ones. In this way, anger would feature as a complex feeling elicited by other simpler emotions, such as envy, confusion, craving, and anxiety.

The following is the list of the whole emotional rainbow proposed by the researchers, and I want you to highlight the feelings that you feel describe you as a person when imagining different circumstances.

- admiration
- adoration
- aesthetic appreciation
- amusement
- anxiety
- awe
- awkwardness
- boredom
- calmness
- confusion
- craving
- disgust
- empathetic pain
- entrancement
- envy
- excitement
- fear
- horror
- interest
- joy

- nostalgia
- romance
- sadness
- satisfaction
- sexual desire
- sympathy
- triumph

Ideally, this exercise should make you aware of the complexity of your emotional array and teach you to be more supportive and compassionate with yourself. It is perfectly okay to be confused about your own feelings, and your anger outbursts are a direct consequence of such confusion. Take more time to analyze your inner self and never ignore your feelings!

3

KNOW YOUR TRIGGERS

"I lose my temper, but it's all over in a minute," said the student. "So is the hydrogen bomb," I replied. "But think of the damage it produces!"

— GEORGE SWEETING

In chapter 1, we briefly covered the importance of recognizing your triggers. This chapter will address the topic of triggers in a more exhaustive way. You will learn that these typical elements at the base of an anger outburst can be of different natures and can be used in productive ways.

"TRIGGERED" ISN'T JUST A BUZZWORD

We have understood that triggers are cues in the environment that will elicit a particular response in the individual experiencing them. To explain anger triggers, we must first refer to the *evolutionary perspective*.

According to such a perspective, an anger response is elicited when an individual experiences frustration over the accomplishment of a given aim. This frustration is generally caused by abstractions. If you set a goal and there is an obstacle to your achievement of that goal, you will feel frustration over your powerlessness and get angry at that specific obstacle. In the animal world, these impediments would generally concern two primary domains: competition over prey and competition over loving partners. However, there are also items of "affection" to consider; a lioness would instantly kill any other animal or human attempting to get close to her cubs.

In our modern society, there exist many forms of impediments and obstacles to our goal of self-fulfillment. Our current social struggles, as women, make up a great deal of our anger triggers. We have talked about the high frequency of workplace sexual harassment and the feeling of frustration elicited when we are being labeled as "too emotional," where any attempt of anger expression is silenced and dismissed. These are all impediments to our personal fulfillment, which go beyond the mere survival instinct of animals.

In the savage world, even the weakest animal would react with rage if a possibility of escape is not provided. This is very much reflected in the human world. A woman who sees an imminent menace (maybe an assault, a theft) and sees no way to escape, will react with rage and anger to protect herself, even if the assailant is a stronger man. This is an important feature that evolution has given us because it enables our systems to fight for our survival even when the weighted chances of success are very low.

Overall, we have identified two important domains where anger triggers can assist us: they can serve us as *threat/obstacle detectors*, but they also give us the drive to *react*. Otherwise, why would we detect them in the first place?

Here is where our society's gender gap gives us more problems. If triggers are perceived dangers and obstacles to our personal fulfillment, then why do we encounter so many difficulties in expressing them? Awareness is needed over this topic such that anger can be recognized as a physiological tool evolved to assist every individual in modern society. It functions as a point of reflection to determine whether our core beliefs and values are being respected in the outer world. This means that anger triggers are not only primordial and primitive instincts that assist with our bare survival, but they were also developed simultaneously to our ethics system, which makes us differentiate between what is right from what is wrong, according to our opinions.

However, it is very complicated to provide a straightforward definition of what a trigger is when it comes to anger. This is because these triggers can also be elicited by other things, which do not necessarily meet our descriptions. More than half of the anger reported by individuals are triggered by internal feelings, rather than having contingent external references, thus showing that anger most of the time occurs in a non-social context (Kashdan and colleagues, 2015).

So, where does it come from? It probably has its roots somewhere inside of you, and it is buried too deep for you to be able to easily detect it. This could be the trace of a trauma you survived in your childhood, an unconscious phobia, or unresolved matters that you had archived thinking they would be unharmful. The understanding and resolution of these triggers requires a lot of attention be paid to these traumatic events and, in most cases, requires the intervention of a professional figure.

We have extensively talked about what triggers are and why they exist, so now we will shift our attention to understanding how our brains use them to warn us about future events.

Your brain uses a lot of resources and energies to warn us of dangers and obstacles, so it also needs to make sure that we learn from them. Ideally, when your brain triggers you to anticipate a given aversive event, it also requires you to develop a strategy to overcome it, so you will not need to go through the whole escalation cycle all over again. Can you recall feeling extremely tired after a bad anger outburst? You might have felt completely drained of energy and physically exhausted. This is because every time you experience an anger outburst your brain employs a great amount of epinephrine and norepinephrine, to enable you "survive" the rage episode.

The epinephrine is released by adrenal glands to enable the amygdala to communicate with frontal lobes and let them know you are getting angry. The norepinephrine assists you during decision-making, giving you the resources to best deal with the situation of danger. These chemicals are nothing more than an adrenaline rush, which is very tiring for your body. So how does your brain make sure that, in the future, you will be able to detect your triggers on time without having to go through such energy consumption all over again? It does so through the creation of a "memory trace."

The first time that a given anger episode occurs, your brain will detect little hints in the environments that will function as warning triggers in the future. The first time the event occurs you should have ideally developed a strategy of how to escape the danger or overcome it, so that the next time you feel triggered and possible recurrence of that event, you will be prepared to react accordingly. For you to understand that an analogous event is about to occur, your brain will make you feel the same emotions and feelings you felt the first time.

The following chapter will explain in detail how this occurs relative to anger triggers. The mechanism of memory tracing has elicited a lot of interest in many research fields, as well as occupying an honorable position in the marvelous *In Search of Lost Time* by Marcel Proust.

In a passage of the *Swann's Way*, the first volume of the whole work, Proust describes an event of himself eating a sweet that suddenly made him feel an unexpected emotion. The sweet, famous madeleine was the trigger of the remembrance of a past event. In Proust's case, the event was positive because the feelings he described were cheerful and overwhelmingly good. In the case of anger, the feelings are very different, but the mechanism is the same.

COMMON ANGER TRIGGERS

What are the main triggers of your anger? Based on the previous definitions of triggers as being perceived threats, you might imagine them to be external cues of different nature, and you are not entirely wrong. If in the past, you have experienced a particularly upsetting event, your brain has probably encoded some relevant cues as a protective measure for your future self. Among the most common external anger triggers, we find elements such as songs, movies, news articles, smells, places, a time of the day, or a day of the year. These are all things that are generally regarded as part of life, but to a person that is triggered by any of them, even the slightest hint could remind them of a particular memory of anger.

Triggers bring you back in time to the moment when the unpleasant event took place, and make you relive those same feelings to avoid the same situation repeating itself. Bear in mind, however, that the triggers are not the reasons for which you felt anger, but rather background elements that your brain captured to form an outline of the situation in your memory.

Picture the scenario where you are having a bad argument with your partner, and you get extremely angry at them. While you two are shouting and fighting, the song "Girl, You'll Be a Woman Soon" by Urge Overkill is playing softly in the background. Your brain will most likely register that song in association with your anger feeling, and when you hear it in the future you might feel the same anger you experienced during the fight. But your brain has not necessarily registered the song, it has most likely only done so if the element of playing music represented a difference in your immediate environment. In a few words, this means that your brain will ignore common elements in the environment to which you are accustomed; it will not register the clock tick, the intermittent light of the fire alarm, or the centrifuge of your washing machine that you hear every day. These stimuli are irrelevant and would not be good cues for you to remember a relevant episode. Thus, your brain will pick on unexpected cues or stimuli, such as the bell ring of an unscheduled visit, a song that you only rarely listen to, or the fire alarm itself should it go off in that moment.

However, what are the chances that during a fight one of these improbable events will happen? What will your brain focus on to register as a trigger for your future warning? It could be anything that already has an emotional value to you. During the fight you might be see your dog assuming a particular position, or maybe your beloved picture on the wall stands out to you at that moment. You could also be noticing unusual modifications of random objects: a stain on your couch, a scratch on your tv screen, the fridge left open. Your brain could register anything that it deems important in that moment to use as a cue to remind you of that event. It will metaphorically say to you, "The next time you hear this song, see that stain on the couch, or look at this particular picture on the wall, you will suddenly remember this event, and therefore experience the feelings associated with it."

HOW TO IDENTIFY YOUR PERSONAL TRIGGERS

From our analysis of triggers, it emerges that they can simply be elements of the environment or feelings within you. But now that you think of an anger event, you cannot remember any outstanding cue that your brain has registered as a trigger. You also don't understand how to isolate particular feelings and directly associate them to that event. Frustration, sadness, and disappointment can be caused by these sorts of reminders; they weren't always the cause for an anger outburst during your life.

The key message to takeaway is this: You are not a machine, and your brain is not necessarily wired in a unidirectional manner. You are complex and multi-layered, and you are not supposed to constantly keep track of what happens inside of you. Therefore, even getting a glimpse of a single phenomenon taking place in our brain requires dedication, effort, and study.

This book will now suggest a few simple steps to help you understand your personal triggers.

First, try to keep track of your physical and emotional changes when you feel a shift occurring in any circumstance or interaction. Do not ignore slight signs of emotional distress, such as annoyance and physical anguish. When I was at university, I had to give a presentation to members of my class and professor. I am a naturally anxious person and have difficulty speaking in public settings. On the day of the presentation, I tried to convince myself that the classroom where we were to present would be small and the audience made up of very few people. However, when I entered the room, the situation was very different. I saw a larger audience made up of multiple professors and students from other class times as well. I immediately had a bodily response due to the shock, and even though I tried to suppress it, I ultimately had a panic attack. To avoid this situation in the future, I could recognize the feeling of anxiety and fear of public speaking prior to the event and try to soothe myself by employing techniques I know would help me calm down. If you were to experience a similar scenario, a good solution would be to acknowledge your state and engage in relaxation techniques such as deep breathing and meditation. These techniques can prepare you for a triggering event and minimize the risk of catastrophic results.

It is important for you to always acknowledge your triggers so that you will be able to recognize them when they reappear in your life.

Overall, a good way to recognize your triggers could be paying attention to your inner self as well as to changes in your breath and heart rate, stomach and chest sensations, and general perception changes because these might be the signs of an anxiety or anger attack. Once you have overcome the moment, always take your time to rationally process what has occurred to you. Try to create a mental map where you trace back triggers, causes, reactions, and consequences.

MOVING PAST YOUR TRIGGERS

Is it possible to heal from triggers? Usually, a trigger can be considered as resolved when its occurrence does not cause you any reaction.

Think of the instance where you have just broken up with your partner, but you still have friends in common or your town is little. You might then casually meet your ex in the streets, and the first few times, it feels to you as a punch in the stomach. You are probably hurt and angry about your breakup, and you wish you hadn't seen them at all.

However, you will find that time heals pain, and while that may not be a comfort to you in the moment, you will get progressively more indifferent when you see that person or remember that past hurt. This doesn't mean you have erased your memories with them, it just means that such memories are not bound to any negative emotional values anymore. When this instance takes place, you have successfully healed from a trigger.

In this case, the trigger was unexpectedly seeing your ex and causing emotional distress. In a similar situation, the best way to process the trigger is doing a deep awareness exercise, which we will cover shortly. In essence, you would need to accept the fact that you cannot avoid seeing that person, and you would have to work in detaching from them any negative emotional value. However, there are many other circumstances where this process is much harder and will require more time and patience.

As we have mentioned before, you might not even be aware of your triggers, and the first step to doing so is systematically identifying them by employing deep personal analysis. Only then will you be able to reprogram your negative thoughts and strengthen your mind with a positive set of core ideals that would prevent you from being triggered.

HORMONAL IMBALANCE AS TRIGGERS

But what happens if you are looking for your trigger in the wrong place? You might be doing well "naming your anger," but you just cannot find useful hints to localize your anger. This might be a good time to talk to your therapist or doctor, because you could either be affected by deep-rooted triggers that require more psychological attention, or you are potentially suffering from hormonal imbalances.

There are many root causes for hormonal imbalances in women. One of the leading causes of elevated mood swings in women is excessive stress, which can be caused by a variety of different things: a bad day at work, many things to handle at home, pressure, responsibilities, and so on. We have seen how this factor is very present in women affected by anger management issues. When it's particularly hard to localize your anger, you might consider yourself to be suffering from excessive stress. However, it is almost never so straightforward and simple; thus, it is always better to consult a professional in the field. Why would stress be involved in anger? When you are stressed, your adrenal glands secrete adrenaline and cortisol.

Adrenaline is the same chemical released during an anger outburst, and when you are stressed you are experiencing the same bodily responses as when you detect a perceived danger. Your fight or flight response system activates, and the rest of your system is put on hold. This might cause your stomach to bloat and you to experience anger. If you experience longer periods of stress, you might also face other consequences, based on how your body responds to cortisol. You might lose or gain weight and experience constant mood swings, from anger to depression.

Another extremely common cause of irrational anger episodes in women is the hormonal imbalance caused by premenstrual syndrome (PMS). According to scientific reports, 75% of women in their reproductive phase experience this condition, while a smaller percentage experience extremely severe PMS symptoms (Alwafa et al., 2021). Some of you might, indeed, relate to those feelings of extreme restlessness, anger, and irritation alternated with episodes of low mood, depression, and sadness. All this is exacerbated by the typical physical pain (muscle tension, back pain) that precedes menstruation. These abrupt mood changes are caused by hormonal imbalances that are typical of this period. In fact, the days preceding menstruation are characterized by a progressive increase of estrogen to prepare the body for ovulation and are followed by an increase of progesterone. When the release of these hormones is further complicated by low levels of serotonin, you might experience symptoms of irritability and anger. If you are unsure that you suffer from PMS, try to keep track of your symptoms in correspondence to your ovulation cycle. Maybe you are confused about how you feel, and you only recall experiencing such mood swings during an indefinite time of the month. In the case in which you belong to that 75%, it would be worth talking to your doctor who can suggest you use hormonal birth control or natural remedies, based on your unique circumstances.

Another syndrome affecting the 10% of women (*Premenstrual Dysphoric Disorder: Symptoms & Treatment*, 2020) is the so-called premenstrual dysphoric disorder (PMDD). It is a more severe form of PMS, the causes of which are not well understood. The hormonal bases are still linked to premenstrual disbalances, but the particular interaction with serotonin plays a role which is still a matter of debate. The symptoms of this syndrome are more debilitating than simply PMS. Along with mood swings and the prevalence of anger feelings, women affected by this condition usually experience physical distress, such as bloating, food cravings, insomnia, and a lot of fatigue. The emotional imbalances are also much worse and more pronounced than those experienced with PMS. Women affected by PMDD might experience very bad depressive episodes causing suicidal thoughts, alternated with very severe anger and panic attacks. Because of its severity, anger management exercises can be useful but need to be accompanied by other treatment interventions designed by your doctor. Among possible treatments we can find the prescription of antidepressants to regulate serotonin levels, painkillers to help with physical premenstrual pain, as well as stress and anger management tools.

MENOPAUSE AS A TRIGGER

If you are not in your reproductive phase anymore but experience similar symptoms as PMS, you might be affected by another condition very typical of your age.

You might be experiencing mood swings due to menopause. It is very common for women in menopause to experience anger attacks, as well as other mood irregularities. This is because, while your body has been used to producing certain amounts of hormones for the majority of your life, it is now confronted with a radical change. Estrogen is the main hormone regulating reproduction, and the approach of menopause significantly slows down its production. How is this related to anger issues? Well, estrogen also regulates the levels of serotonin produced (the "happy" chemical of your brain); thus, the reduction of one might cause the reduction of the other. Besides abstract speeches on various hormones and their balances, you might also rationally know the roots of your anger related to menopause: Many women lose their self-esteem when they reach menopause, feeling as if they are getting older. At this stage, they might not feel confident about their bodies and self-worth. However, this problem, like any other in life, has its solutions. Once you have made sure to suffer from menopausal mood changes, there are several remedies that could help you regain control of your mood. Physical exercise, for example, could stimulate the production of endorphins. Exercises like Pilates and cardio can help you regain confidence in your body, as well as lowering the chances of getting cardiovascular diseases.

Balancing your diet might also help you regulate your hormone levels. In fact, the lowering of estrogen also causes the weakening of your bones, and foods rich in calcium, iron, and vitamin D will help you feel both emotionally and physically better.

However, it is not always so easy and immediate to get the help we deserve, mostly because there is little education about hormonal imbalances in women, especially those due to perimenopause.

An example of a similar circumstance is provided by the story of Teri Hines, a woman who experienced perimenopausal symptoms and was ignored for several years (Chatterjee, 2020). Teri, as she approached her mid-40s, started to experience episodes of anxiety and low mood, which caused her to struggle to get up from bed and go to work. As she was living alone, she started withdrawing from friends and spent more and more time in solitude. Whenever she would talk to her doctor, he would tell her that her symptoms were typical of her age and generally do nothing to help her. In this way, she started cohabiting with her symptoms, thinking they would go away with time. She only started taking her situation more seriously when she realized that her symptoms persisted, even after several years. She then had the strength and self-awareness to go back to her doctor and tell him she was clearly suffering from depression. Only then did he prescribe her antidepressants, and she learned how to recognize her triggers on time. Among her most relevant triggers, there are some that I believe to be very common in women of her age. In fact, this age period is generally affected by several life changes, such as career boosts or declines, relationships "shocks" (maybe a divorce or perhaps your son or daughter leaving home, etc.), and others. Hence, besides the difficulties that a woman faces in this period because of hormonal disbalances, they might also have to go through the pressure exercised by drastic life changes.

As a constant in this book, it is always pivotal for you to be able to recognize the features of your life stages and possible triggers that might affect your normal life. When you feel unsure about your mental and physical health it is always a good idea to talk to others, either by speaking with your close ones or seeking professional help.

EMPOWER YOURSELF WITH SELF-IDENTIFICATION

Exercise 1: Defining My Triggers

As we have understood in this chapter, triggers have a common physiological basis for all but essentially change from person to person. It is then necessary that you master the ability to recognize some or all your triggers, and the exercise below might help you to do so.

First, try to identify your general struggles and problems. If you suffer from anger attacks, you might think that anger is the trigger itself. However, most often, anger is the emotion through which your inner triggers are expressed, and, if unmanaged, it might cause you several difficulties in your relationships with society. Common struggles associated with anger issues are difficulties in concentrating and multitasking, for example. As we have seen that anger generally distracts attention from all other things unrelated to it, it is not uncommon to find it difficult to concentrate on your work, for instance. Now, this is the space for you to think about the struggles you encounter during your day-to-day life and list them all on a piece of paper.

After having done that, try to focus on elements belonging to different categories that might function as triggers for you. Think of any person, place, emotional state, or thought that, when encountered, has caused you an angry reaction in the past. Now, do you think the problems you have listed occur more often when one of the triggers identified is unleashed? Maybe you have noticed that you are more stressed at work when a specific coworker has a shift with you. Or maybe you realized that every time you go to the mall or other crowded places, you feel angrier or in distress. In this way, this exercise could help you point out particular anger-cause-consequences patterns that, if analyzed and disentangled, could help you resolve some of your triggers.

Exercise 2: Triggers Journal

Another exercise I would like to propose to help you manage your anger triggers is to utilize a diary or journal. Because of the shame and guilt you might feel after an anger attack, your immediate instinct could be to forget everything. To "just forget it" is also a piece of common advice we might receive from an inexperienced friend who is trying to help. However, if you forget or ignore your mistakes you will never learn from them. For this reason, it could be helpful to write down as many details as you can about your anger attack before it gets forgotten.

Because you might want to do it when you feel angry or after you have just exploded, you might find it hard to write down long and concise phrases. That is okay. It is also okay to frantically take notes of words that, in that moment, you think better describe your mental state. These can be descriptions of feelings, places, people, or anything you deem important in that moment. As you write you will notice that you progressively calm down; it could be a good moment to force yourself to put all those words together to form more coherent phrases. This is important because if you attempted to read those notes on a different day you would struggle to make sense, and all your struggles of writing would be in vain.

It will be difficult at first, but over time, you will find this exercise enlightening, and you will be surprised at the level of introspection this task could help you gain for yourself.

4

GET TO THE ROOT CAUSE

Patience and empathy are anger's mortal enemies.

— GARY RUDZ

Up to this point we have talked about anger as a protective and evolutionary emotion. It exists so we can detect threats in a social context, but it also functions as a tool to constantly verify that the external world is in accordance with our inner ethics. But anger is also a very complex emotion, and most of us struggle when it comes to having conscious control over it. It is usually the contrary: anger takes control and has the power of making us violent, raging, and primordial for the period in which it is experienced. But does it really function as a switch? Are we truly cheerful and happy one moment and angry and violent the moment after? Our brain is more complex than that, and it is influenced by both chemical and environmental causes. This is an indicator that anger is deeply rooted inside of us and that its arousal requires a more thorough analysis than we initially thought.

Anger being a complex emotion is not a new concept, as it is ascertained that anger makes us unreliable observers and narrators, it controls our attention and actions, and it is not a simple mechanism that can be easily unwired. What happens when anger intertwines with other deep-rooted emotions like feelings of sadness, betrayal, unworthiness, and hurt? Do we first need to unlock those emotions to then be able to free ourselves from the anger on which they feed?

Let us have a look at how anger is related to other grounded emotions and how they mutually benefit from each other.

WHAT ARE YOUR EMOTIONS REALLY TELLING YOU?

We have talked about anger as being physiologically similar to anxiety, sharing the common features of adrenaline release and the fight or flight response. Anger has a symbiotic relationship with depression; one feeds on the other and vice versa. The serotonergic imbalance that is typical of depressed individuals is what causes the feelings of melancholy and sadness that we are all familiar with. But this emotional pattern does not necessarily exclude a role played by anger, such that medications used to treat depression also contribute to treating symptoms of anger. It is very common for depressed individuals to exhibit symptoms of repressed anger. This, in turn, has a negative effect on depression, as repressing your anger if you already suffer from depression, can worsen the feelings of low confidence and self-worth.

Depression can take many forms, and if you are having trouble controlling your anger, there might be a good chance that you suffer from depression too. This is because a typical side effect of depression is being irritable and more susceptible to external triggers. Reactions caused by angry and depressed individuals include anger outbursts, irrational reactions, and not being able to adapt reactions to social contexts. It is important to be able to correctly detect anger when it is paired with depression because treating one while ignoring the other does not lead to any positive outcome.

Specifically tailored to treat angry depression, there is a psychological intervention called Emotionally Focused Therapy which differentiates between adaptive and non-adaptive anger. According to this therapy's viewpoint, the *non-adaptive anger* (anger for anger, not with a motivating purpose) needs to be transformed into *adaptive anger* (anger that creates motivation).

For example, if a depressed individual is mulling over their issues with doing well at school or university, the depressive aspect would contribute to worsening self-perception and the non-adaptive anger would make them hostile to other people that they deem to be smarter. This would only cause a vicious cycle where the person hates themselves and others and finds no way to get back to the surface. On the other hand, when the anger is turned into adaptive anger, the depressed individual is trained to take action to change their negative inner voice. In the case of low self-esteem at school, the person would learn to motivate themselves, study more, and try to find a bigger-picture mindset to help them understand that they always tend to see others better than themselves. Once contingent progressions are noticed (better grades at school, healthier outlook), then the person would also make progressions with the symptoms of depression.

"Why am I so angry?" When we ask ourselves this question, we tend to give fuzzy answers and avoid getting straight to the point. We might attribute our anger to the bad weather, our failure in succeeding with something, or maybe a bad day at work. But when it comes to acknowledging the bad that someone close has done to us, many of us tend to be hesitant. It is not easy to acknowledge and even realize that we might be angry because we have been betrayed by a close friend, a partner, or a parent.

Maybe this betrayal traces back to when you were young or several years back, and for this reason, you tend to assume that such an event was forgotten. However, you might still be suffering from the consequences of never internally processing the betrayal. This feeling can be considered a loss, like the one we experience when a person we love passes away. However, there is a fundamental difference between loss by death and loss by betrayal. We learn to process death and its consequences from the time we are children: We theoretically know that people will one day die, and we constantly, although unconsciously, prepare ourselves for the future occurrence of death. Yet we tend not to consider that we might lose someone because we have been betrayed. To betray someone is a personal choice. It requires the person to know how to hurt us (by knowing our life history, our opinions, and feelings), and this element makes the person, most of the time, unforgivable. So how does anger find its way through betrayal?

Betrayal, like any other negative emotion, needs to be processed to avoid detrimentally affecting us. When betrayal is not processed, that feeling of loss inside of us might transform into resentment and anger. We might react aggressively to strangers trying to befriend us because unconsciously we might fear being betrayed again. However, if we don't know these deep-rooted reasons for our anger, we might wrongly label ourselves as naturally irritable. Acknowledging the betrayal is the first step to moving past it. Next, a good healing process could be identifying some key activities that could help you vent the anger. These could be physical exercise, writing down your feelings, or anything that you would usually do to release your energy.

Let us now cover a very important and common aspect when it comes to anger. If this emotion can be the expression of hidden feelings (like in the case of betrayal) or of comorbidities (depression, anxiety), it can also be a phenomenon that we all have heard of at least once: post-traumatic stress disorder (PTSD). PTSD is a mental disease caused by the occurrence of a terrifying, hurtful, and traumatic event. When something terrifying happens (think of the explosion of a bomb, a natural disaster, a sexual assault, severe fights between your parents when you were a child, and so on), your brain will recruit all its healing capacities to move past it, but when the event was too shocking, it may generally require the intervention of a professional figure.

Anger is very much related to trauma and can be an important symptom to recognize the condition. According to the DSM-5 (Diagnostic and Statistical Manual of Mental Disorders, 5th Edition), to diagnose PTSD the individual must exhibit at least two symptoms showing increased arousal and hyperactivity, and one symptom showing a pattern of avoidance. These two elements together are usually exhibited as overt aggression and irritability, as well as being very suspecting of other people. The neurobiology of trauma, as well, is very similar to anger, such that the initially perceived threat (that triggers the trauma) is stored in the amygdala as a memory with emotional content, but because of the excessive emotional response, the elevated cortisol that is secreted shuts down the communication between the hippocampus and neocortex—which is responsible for the correct storage of an event in long-term memory. This means that the event will never be time-processed: You would not be able to store the memory of the event in a temporal and contextual manner and, in this way, when you are triggered, you will relive the moment as if it is occurring in the present. The expression of anger is very common in this context because the brain does not know any other useful way to protect you in a similar situation. Trauma focused CBT is a very common treatment used to heal PTSD, focused on processing the trauma and placing it in its temporal context.

ANGER AND GENDER INEQUALITIES

Can gender inequalities be the direct cause of mental illness in women? According to Jane Leonard (2021), the answer is yes. Gender inequalities are socio-economic and political injustices caused by sexism that continue to occur in a variety of different contexts. These include inequalities in working environments and salaries, schooling and employment, and higher dangers of sexual harassment. Women are always more likely to be victims of these inequalities, and the consequences include mental illness. In fact, women are twice as likely to develop symptoms of generalized anxiety disorder, depression, eating disorders, and PTSD. Do you think that PTSD could be a bit extreme to mention among the consequences of gender inequalities? Well, then you are certainly not thinking about the higher rates of genitalia mutilation, childhood marriage, partner abuse, and backstreet abortions (in countries where it is not legal) affecting women worldwide.

When it comes to women's bodies and the policing of their standards, society always has something to say. We will now briefly mention the matter of eating disorders and body dysmorphia. Society has been confronted with gender stereotypes since the first glimpse of humankind on earth. In ancient Greece, women were very much confined to the roles of mothers and nurturers, which still occurs today in several societies. The introduction of social networks has been jeopardizing women's mental health and self-esteem with its sole focus on algorithms that popularize certain feminine ideals. Instagram, for example, has gained so much popularity in the last decade due to one fundamental feature: It allows ordinary people to have constant updates on celebrities' lives. We are constantly exposed to the view of wealthy women with "perfect" bodies, tons of properties, tons of friends, and an apparently perfect life. We watch their stories and witness their growing popularity and we unconsciously pair their beauty with their social position. Nowadays, the beauty standard imposes big lips, hourglass body shape, and tanned or healthy skin. An image that is not inclusive of the myriad of women's body types, not even of the vast majority of them.

However, it is important to realize that none of what we watch is natural, and this is an important message spread by the famous individuals who raise awareness and remove the veil on how these "ideal" bodies are made. Unnaturally full lips are the results of plastic surgery, that flawless hourglass body shape is the result of hours and hours spent at the gym (and plastic surgery), and that tanned and healthy skin is very much provided by the wonders of photoshop. However, when we are confronted with such "perfection," we cannot stop comparing our bodies to those of the women we see having more success than us. This inevitably causes anger and frustration and, unfortunately, eating disorders and psychological conditions that require special attention.

If you are a victim of this societal pressure, take a step back from social media to identify what truly makes you feel beautiful. It is important to not rely on external standards that are modeled to constrict women's expectations and definition of what is beautiful.

LETTING GO OF PAST HURT TO HEAL THE PRESENT

Getting to the roots of your feelings is always key to understanding and changing your actions in the world. In this chapter, we have understood that simply forcing yourself to change a given behavior does not address the problem at its core and, most of all, does not prevent it from happening again. Your anger outbursts might be the expression of deeper disturbances that might be hard to recognize, specifically because they are hidden by your frequent aggressive behavior. However, venting your anger on external targets does not heal your internal wounds. Acting with violence in your everyday life will not treat your depression or feeling of betrayal; on the contrary, it will bury those root causes even more deep down, until they will be too far away to get back to the surface in their raw form. The process of "letting go" includes both acknowledging and releasing the bad energies enclosed in a given feeling. Once you have identified an emotion such as hurt due to betrayal, try to isolate it from the rest of your emotional spectrum and focus on that feeling. You will notice several changes within you, and you will be able to attribute those changes directly to that feeling.

Following such acknowledgment, you should then do some activities to let go of your pain. These can be like crying out. If you feel like you are so hurt that crying is the only spontaneous action that can follow, do not contain yourself. Crying always forms part of the healing process, and missing this step could worsen your situation and build further stress and anger. You could try to channel your sadness into positive actions which is always a good solution as it employs your pain in a productive way. Engaging your energy in something you have control over is a good way to release your bad energies into the external world.

The Story of Laurie Christopher

Laurie Christopher is a woman who has suffered from debilitating mental and physical conditions throughout her life, yet she is the leading example of strength and resilience.

Laurie has lived a traumatic childhood: Her mother was a drug addict and her father left them very early. Her mother started having casual relationships with different men until she found a long-lasting partner. This partner, a violent drug addict himself, was constantly beating up Laurie and her brother, whom she says was her greatest hero. The little brother would be the only person standing between the angry man and Laurie, but, when he moved out of that toxic environment, for Laurie, there was no escape. Her stepdad started sexually assaulting her, and he and her mother were occasionally trading little Laurie to other men for drugs. Laurie reported to have lived this life until the age of 15 when she escaped. She ran away from home, and, lying about her age, she found a job and started a new life. She progressively found better jobs as she grew up and slowly acquired her independence. However, her old life did not disappear from her persona; it was still a part of her and was constantly influencing her imminent future. As an adult, Laurie reported having no memories of her childhood, and the only expressions of her traumatic past were recurrent nightmares, outbursts of anger and crying, depression, and general symptoms of PTSD. Only after starting to work with a neuropsychologist and clinical psychologist, did her memories slowly start to come back to surface. Her first memory successfully retrieved was the image of her sitting in the backseat of a stranger's car, whom she then recalled being the man to whom she was traded for drugs.

Laurie learned about the importance of letting go and allowing oneself to be free of past pains. Her psychologist helped her retrieve all her memories, identify key feelings associated with them, and suggested activities tailored to address her specific problem. She learned how to forgive herself from the guilt and shame she unconsciously felt. She slowly regained power over herself and built a connection of trustworthy people to regain confidence in building relationships with others. If Laurie managed to get back on track with her life, all of us can. There is always a solution, even for those among us who have gone through unimaginable pain.

EMPOWER YOURSELF WITH SELF-FREEDOM

Exercise 1: Letting Go

Having very much focused on the topic of letting go, this exercise is specifically tailored to develop your skills on releasing yourself from resentment.

Every time that you are holding on to something (a feeling of anger or frustration) which prevents you from letting go of your negative feelings, there is always an element of resentment at its roots.

For this exercise, try to focus on events that might even have occurred far away in your past. Instead of searching for anger triggers that occurred in your past working week, try to look back to when you were a child or teenager. You might suddenly remember past jealousy (maybe as a child you felt that your brother or sister was getting more attention than you), fights with your parents of which you never really understood the reasons, and so on.

Now, as it is always better to do when working on rage, try to write down on a piece of paper the reasons for your resentments that you have identified.

Also, write down how, according to you, the specific person *should have* behaved differently, working in this way towards the resolutions of your resentments.

Take an objective look at the situation: Identify your role in the situation by analyzing how you behaved and trying to identify potential reasons for which that person behaved that way. Maybe you were being unreasonable, or maybe your core beliefs and values did not fully agree with those of the given person.

It is always important to consider several perspectives of the same situation of injustice, because only through comprehending the reasons for your actions and the other person's actions can you let go of resentment.

5

SELF-CARE AND THE POWER OF MINDFULNESS

It is wise to direct your anger towards problems—not people; to focus your energies on answers—not excuses.

— WILLIAM ARTHUR WARD

THE IMPORTANCE OF SELF-CARE

In light of what we have discussed so far, what are the best ways to channel your anger into positive emotions?

First, as I will stress throughout this book, always take a moment to find the reasons for which you are feeling so angry. This will help you calm down, not because you are told to do so, but because you are training your body into understanding its limits. The first time will probably be hard because training your brain can be as difficult as growing muscles at the gym or mastering your favorite sport.

Imagine your worst anger attack and go back in your memory to picture how you reacted to those triggers. You were probably outraged, and certainly, you would not imagine yourself just stopping screaming and regaining your calm in a couple of seconds. Do not forget the power of naming something: It will take its own form and identity and will be more likely to be remembered.

Try to write down on a piece of paper a list of activities that make you feel calmed and relaxed. The next time you have an anger attack you should focus on that list and commit to one of those activities. If you are unsure about what might be a good activity or feel like those you have identified do not really work, there are some general relaxing activities that should work for everybody. According to Erica Cirino (2018) and backed up by the Psychologist Timothy J. Legg, examples of such tasks are: learning how to breathe, picturing yourself in a calm situation, physical exercise, and focusing on exiting the anger thinking loop. The activities you have identified will be the ones you will have to start doing once you have managed to calm down from an anger episode.

In anger management, self-care always matters. Taking care of yourself means acknowledging your worth and value, which is key to learning how to deal with your emotions. There are not universal examples of self-care activities, because they might include anything that would make you feel happy and rewarded. If you like cooking, dedicating some time of the day to that activity would be beneficial. Similarly, if you are a sporty person, going for a run or walk once a day could definitely ameliorate your mood.

Have you ever battled with the idea that taking any time for yourself to take care of yourself seems selfish? You have an infinite number of responsibilities and people to look after in your life. Perhaps taking any time for yourself is not something you have ever had time to contemplate. Since you have come this far in the book, there is a secret you should know. You already set self-care as one of your priorities in life, and you should be proud! To me, selfishness is not protecting what you have and who you are by carving out time to invest in the things that bring you joy or keep your emotional and mental well-being balanced and in a good place. That is self-care. Selfishness is pulling someone else along to validate that what you are endeavoring to do is self-care, when you do not need that outside opinion to know what your instincts are yelling at you. There is a reason all those idioms are repeated time and time again. "Make sure you secure your own mask over your face on a plane before you help someone else." "Learn to love yourself before you love someone else." For those of us who have prioritized other's care before our own, you listen to this wisdom but know you do not heed it. Now, more than ever, you know that self-care is a crucial aspect of your anger management journey because if you were missing the "excuse" to do so before, you have permission to take time for yourself to identify those activities that bring you joy or keep you at peace. It is your duty to build up a system that perpetuates good habits and behavior, and what better incentive is there than doing something that will make you feel good, feel whole, feel grounded?

An example of what I do for self-care is knitting. At the risk of sounding young and naïve, it truly is no longer a craft that should be relegated as something to take up when you are older or have grandchildren. (Though that is one of the best times to do so, because I have heard that grandchildren are very happy to play with yarn if you can teach them to hand-knit, which is knitting with nothing more than yarn and their little hands.) One of my pearls of wisdom when it comes to self-care is that using your hands can be very therapeutic and a great way to lull your restless mind with a mindless craft you can do almost unconsciously after a bit of practice. Whether you decide to do another making craft like pottery, sewing, cross-stitching, crocheting, knitting, or put your hands in the dirt and start gardening, you are essentially cultivating something of your very own that would not be in existence if you did not decide to pick up a set of needles, a crochet hook, or a shovel.

Regardless of the activity you choose to engage in, you always look at the bigger picture: Everyone's bigger picture is the sociohistorical context in which they live every day. The current society imposes a very fast-paced rhythm where most of our daily hours are spent on being economically productive. Whether you are a working woman or not, you are still constantly confronted with a fast-changing environment, which requires constant adaptation and transformation. You need to carve out some valuable time only dedicated to yourself and what makes you happy. Forcing yourself to always be on the top of everything by keeping up with this crazy rhythm can only be detrimental to your physical and mental health.

THE IMPORTANCE OF MINDFULNESS

Mindfulness is a practice that originates from a Buddhist tradition, and its practical application involves meditation techniques from Tibet. It is a very widespread practice and has been employed to treat symptoms of anxiety, depression, stress, and drug addiction. It is largely based on the assumption that being aware of your moment-to-moment state of being (feelings, emotions) without having a judgmental outlook, can be beneficial to the individual. Among the benefits found with the practice of mindfulness is a decrease in rumination and obsessive thinking, as well as the development of strategies and techniques to prevent you from developing mental health problems. Mindfulness can also be considered as a state of mind that you acquire after you train yourself to be aware of your inner self.

A study conducted by David De Steno and colleagues provides evidence for the beneficial effects of mindfulness against anger outbursts. In their experiment, they trained a group of people on mindfulness techniques, such as breathing strategies, focusing on mind and body sensations, and building non-judgmental perspectives on given situations. They then included in the experiment another group that was not trained (the control group), so that they could compare their mindful performance against the trained group. When both groups were then tested on their cognitive and executive functions, they were both given very negative feedback and criticisms, without telling them this was part of the experiment. The anger ratings of the mindful group were significantly lower than those of the control group, showing that mindfulness training successfully decreased the likelihood of getting angry when negatively judged.

According to the researchers, a mindful approach works in a bottom-up manner. For the sake of this topic, we shall now provide a definition of bottom-up vs top-down according to psychological science. Top-down *processing* characterizes all those brain (top) activities involved in the control of cognitive functions to change a behavior (down). This includes focusing on studying or memorizing something, employing memory to remember an episode or being able to do something based on what you learn, and so on.

Bottom-up processing, on the other hand, includes all the external cues (bottom) that are processed by your brain (up) in a given manner. This includes visual processing (a visual stimulus encoded by your brain) and interpretation of sensory information. The fact that mindfulness works in a bottom-up manner means that you don't train your brain into acquiring overt control over your actions, but rather that you wire it in a way that is less sensible of external information. It follows that you are less likely to get angry because you don't consider external cues as threats. Through mindful exercises, you train your brain to feel more compassion rather than drive to revenge, to be less judgmental, and to generally be more Zen, until these characteristics become an integral part of you.

EMPOWER YOURSELF WITH SELF-CARE AND MINDFULNESS

The following exercises are indeed aimed at learning some mindfulness techniques and at understanding how to use them in the most correct and productive way.

The first step in your journey to mindfully take control of your anger is always to recognize its existence. It is important to recognize that anger exists as a part of us and that it doesn't only arise when you are triggered or irritated. It is part of your vast array of emotions and, like all of them, can be employed in a productive or non-productive way. In fact, there is no such thing as a bad emotion. If it exists, it serves a purpose. Even happiness can be detrimental, such that too much of it, and too often, can have you mistakenly labeled as a superficial person, with a poor sense of judgment.

Indeed, we are equipped with such a variety of emotions, so they can help us deal with circumstances of different nature. In this phase, you will focus on your anger's identity and accept its existence as both a negative and positive emotion. There is no point in suppressing your anger; even if you are trying to be in control of a situation in a given moment by containing your anger, it will come back stronger and even more uncontrollable.

The second step towards your successful anger management is to realize that anger is your ally. It does not only exist regardless of our will, but it serves a specific purpose. Now is the time to mentally review all the chapter's content about the anger physiology and our fight or flight response. Looking at anger's positive side is realizing that it is there to warn us of potentially dangerous or detrimental cues in the environment. It activates our instinct of reacting to protect ourselves. When you are walking home late at night and when you feel frustrated at home or work, you should be grateful for your anger. This emotion is signaling to you that something might be potentially dangerous or that you are subject to a situation of injustice.

How to Be in the Moment

Let us now turn to a proper mindfulness technique, which will be useful when the anger inside of us becomes unmanageable.

Now you have accepted that anger exists and that it serves a noble purpose. However, you still experience your horrible anger outbursts—the sensation of your brain and body getting very hot, your heartbeat accelerating, and all that. You still perpetrate your actions following an anger attack. Maybe you are still violent, or you still burst out in tears. How do you stop all that from happening and start channeling your anger into a positive application?

It sounds too simple, but first you must learn how to breathe.

Shortness of breath is, indeed, one of the bodily consequences of an anger outburst. Learning how to breathe in such a moment will also lower your heart rate and help you cool down your brain. Given that you have, by now, learned how to recognize your triggers whenever you spot one in the environment, the first thing you must do is to focus on your breath. Try to withdraw from the event for one moment, applying the objective perspective of which we covered in an earlier section. To do that, you will have to focus on your breath by closing your eyes and repeating to yourself the numbers of your count. Do that until you feel like your body is back to normal.

The following exercises cannot be done every time you find yourself in a situation of anger or danger. These ideally need to be practiced in your safe zone when you have taken some time away from your routine to dedicate a couple of hours for yourself.

During your daily free time, take 10 minutes to practice these mindful exercises. By the time you experience a situation of anger, you will hopefully have mastered some of these techniques, which means that you will have an entirely different perspective on the event.

Now that you are in your safe zone and practicing your breathing technique, begin the following exercise: Stand on your feet, making sure they align with your hips. To do so, your feet will need to be a short distance apart and will be on the same line with your hips and upper body. Then, close your eyes and slightly bend your knees by reaching a squat position (you might want to join your hands in a praying position to achieve better balance). At this point, clear your mind and focus only on the feeling of the floor on the palm of your feet. Think about the floor as a support system for your body and try to withdraw from anything else but this acknowledgment.

After you have found the correct alignment with the floor, thinking about it as a support for your body will result as a natural thing. To then "ground yourself" means finding a balance in that position and feeling comfortable with it. Still by only thinking about the floor under your feet, start taking slow and deep breaths.

Now, try to pay attention to your body sensations. Think about how your skin feels or how your fingertips touch each other and shift your attention to different details of your body. By doing so you have probably become used to that position, and you have forgotten you are squatting. If this position was initially feeling quite uncomfortable, you now feel no different than staying seated on a chair.

If you have successfully reached this point, you should be proud of yourself: You are meditating. You are indeed one step closer to achieving indirect control of your anger, and you are now certainly more aware of your surroundings and yourself in the present moment.

Identify Your Triggers and Name Your Anger

Mindfulness can be employed for a variety of different conditions. It can be used to treat depression, as well as stress and psychosis. In the same way you have focused on your body sensations, now think of anger as an entity and try to make as many associations with it as possible.

Focus on the question "What makes me angry?" and gather all the conclusions you drew from past exercises. Focus on your triggers and try to embed the feeling of anger inside objects and things. If your workplace pops up in your head when you think of anger, then anger will be your office, your coworkers, your boss, and anything related to that environment. In doing so you will progressively think of all the elements that make up your working environment, and you will naturally be drawn toward the real core of your anger. If the trigger is your boss, then you will effortlessly isolate it from all the other elements that do not make you angry. For example, you might initially feel resentment when thinking about your office only because it is directly linked to an element in that environment that causes you stress, your boss for example. By doing this exercise you would ideally find the nucleus of your anger related to that particular environment.

Next, try to name your anger by saying it out loud. You have successfully identified your anger trigger, so all you have to do now is to acknowledge its existence, and, by doing so, you really are isolating your source of anger rather than suppressing it. Having clarified with yourself what makes you angry, you can switch to analyzing your body changing now that you are mentally so close to your anger trigger.

If you feel like you are starting to ruminate or your heartbeat is going faster, this is a good moment to take deep breaths and attempt to rationalize your feelings. Go through the process of analyzing why that makes you angry, how you usually react to it, and the consequences of your actions. Think about all this through an external perspective, as if you were listening to a friend speaking.

The whole point of these exercises is to acquire an external point of view, such that in the future you will not feel so much triggered by what happened in the past. While doing this exercise you can also try to use some fundamental mantras for anger control. As well as focusing on your body sensations, you can try to repeat phrases like "I can do this, I am strong enough," or, "It is what it is," to help you convince yourself that you are calm and Zen, until you actually become calm.

Mindful Affirmations

Mantras can be powerful tools that can accompany you in your journey toward anger management. In the same way you keep in mind useful things for your everyday life, you should take care of your mantras. These can be supportive phrases and encouraging thoughts that you repeat to yourself during stressful times. However, you could also dedicate a time of the day when you meditate by repeating your mantras. By concentrating on the messages you repeat to yourself, these affirmations can really penetrate your core beliefs and values.

If, during the analysis proposed by this book, you have realized that you are a person particularly prone to sadness and low feelings, the mantra you might use could be: "I refuse to allow my sadness overcome my joy."

If, on the other hand, you are more prone to anger outbursts that shock you, given your usual calmer temper, you could opt for something like "I am a calm person, and I refuse to let my anger take control of me."

Your mantras can change every day, based on your mood, your changes of beliefs, and your daily challenges. It is important for you to truly believe in their beneficial power so that they can change the way you think in a valuable way.

Katy Perry and Transcendental Meditation

Katy Perry is one of the most followed pop stars of our generation and, as such, she has a restless lifestyle. Keeping up with similar success is not easy, and being talented, rich, and internationally known are not synonyms of happiness. During several interviews she released, Katy attributed all her life success and ability to overcome daily stress to transcendental meditation.

This form of meditation requires you to quietly sit on the floor with crossed legs (or any position you would find comfortable) for a straight 20-minute session. You would then start deep breathing and repeating your chosen mantras in a loop. This technique can help you go through stress, trauma, anger, and anxiety.

Katy Perry reported having spent at least 20 minutes per day doing meditation since 2011. She usually does it as her first thing in the morning when she is still in bed, but she also does it during different periods of the day when she is particularly stressed. She said that this practice has given her a more Zen approach to life, has filled her with joy and calmness, and that she could not go back to a life with transcendental meditation. Katy is a proper advocate of this practice. She asked her fans to stop giving her gifts but to rather donate to the David Lynch Foundation to raise money to make transcendental meditation accessible to all those people who cannot afford training but need it more than others.

6

COMMUNICATE EFFECTIVELY

You are not the anger; you are the awareness behind the anger. Realize this and the anger will no longer control you.

— ECKHART TOLLE

Until now this book has greatly dealt with the type of work required from you to control your anger issues. The tasks described were mostly suggesting you do solo work to acknowledge your anger, understand your triggers, meditate, and so on. Another fundamental factor when it comes to anger management is to constantly communicate with others.

Life is made of human interactions: We have contact with people from the moment we wake up until when we go to bed. If you want to succeed in this journey, you must first learn how to communicate well with people, from strangers like the grocery store salesperson to your loved ones, like your partner, parents, and children.

EFFECTIVE COMMUNICATION

The Seven Cs of Communication

When you communicate with someone you want to make sure that the person understands what you are saying, so you don't have to repeat yourself multiple times. You also want to tell truthful and reliable information; otherwise, the listener will no longer listen to your words. You also want to be kind and friendly so that the person will have pleasure in talking to you. Overall, communication should be pleasurable and good for you. You surely enjoy speaking with your friends, your partner, or you surely have some key figures in your life with whom you love talking. On the other hand, some other social circumstances might make you insecure and uncomfortable. You might feel you usually have trouble communicating, you feel like listeners judge you, or you are often misunderstood. If this is the case for you, there are some general rules that you should follow to learn how to conduct effective communication.

These rules are called the seven Cs. They are seven words, all starting with the letter C and each providing a sort of commandment.

- **Conciseness** is your first C, and it is there to remind you that, if the idea of having a conversation with someone gives you anxiety, you have to get straight to the point. Try not to be repetitive and try to form your sentences such that they all follow a general structure: pronoun, followed by the main verb, and the direct object.
- **Completeness** is next and suggests you make sure you convey all the information that the listener needs to understand your message. If you must tell your boss he or she has been invited to a meeting, you also want to tell them where, at what time, and with whom. Overall, create a mental schema that helps you remember all the information you have to give so that you can get out of that situation as soon as possible. However, when speaking you also must be considerate of others.
- **Consideration** is your third C. This means that you always have to step in the listener's shoes

and understand that what you know is not what other people know. Your listener might have a different viewpoint, a different vocabulary, and different opinions. When mentally organizing your speech or phrase structure, always ask yourself, "Am I being comprehensible? Will the person understand what I am trying to say?" Do not just assume that the listener has all the information that you have on the matter.
- Be **clear and concrete**, the next two Cs, when speaking. Do not use fuzzy and complex words. Maybe you are soon to have a conversation with someone of whom you don't know the cultural background, and you are not sure at what level of complexity your conversation should be. When in doubt, just be clear by explaining yourself and by using simple words. Just think about the instance where you are giving a presentation (at school or at work). You want to be as clear as possible so that the audience will not stop you while you are speaking, and you are less likely to lose your speech thread. You should think the same when you are having a conversation with a single person because he or she will surely listen to you without interruptions if you are clear enough.

- **Correctness** is your sixth C and reminds you to watch your grammar and style. If you are worried you might make grammatical errors, you could practice that in your own time. If you feel like you have trouble remembering specific verbs or grammatical rules, reviewing them at home could be a good idea. Reading improves your grammatical knowledge and, generally, makes you more comfortable with communication.
- Your seventh C is **Courtesy**, and it reminds you that being kind to others is key to communication. Kindness also ensures you, most of the time, that the listener will be kind as well, regardless of your communication style. Courtesy is also about showing your listener that you are carefully listening and understanding what they are communicating to you. It is a sign of respect and of acknowledgment of the other person's worth.

Tone and Body Language Matters

Communication is not only made of words and verbs, but it also includes all your unconscious body language and voice tone. Have you ever been in a situation where your friend or son/daughter tells you they are feeling good, but their voice tone and body movements say the complete opposite? Certainly yes. This is because our bodies constantly produce movements that are detectable to others and that are made exactly to support communication. So, whenever you are having a bad day but want to hide it, just be aware that it is not as easy as you imagine. Your listener or people around you might gaze at the grudge of your facial expression, may detect a slightly irritated or sad voice tone, as well as your instinctive bodily reflexes; when you are angry you might make more scattered and quick bodily movements.

However, don't think that they are there to judge you. All human beings have evolved to understand body language, ever since they were babies. Think about the fact that body language is the first form of communication we learn as children, even before saying our first words. Hence, it is something we are all very good at by the time we are adults, and there are ways to use this tool in a productive way to boost your communication style.

Indeed, body movements can strengthen your message by making it more compelling: Nodding your head while speaking usually makes your speech more persuasive. Voice tones as well, have developed to communicate at a distance, when direct confrontation is not possible. This is the reason why you might detect your friend's pain and sadness over the phone. Also, the act of gesticulating with your hands usually gives security to the listener, such that they will pay more attention to your words because they understand your intention of explaining. Moreover, do not underestimate the power of gazing. If you want to convey security and self-confidence to your listener, make sure you always keep eye contact. On the other hand, often looking away is a sign of insecurity, so it might be useful for you to keep these precious tips in mind the next time you are having a conversation.

Dealing With Difficult People

Unfortunately, communication is not necessarily immediately easy if you follow those rules. People are not always so easy to deal with, and you will likely be confronted with different personalities every day. Being "difficult" is not a feature of otherness, given that you may consider other people this way simply because they are very different from you. For instance, if you are an introvert, you might bond more easily with shy people; you certainly understand their way of being, and you find more similarities. In this way, you might have more difficulties having a conversation with an extreme extrovert or outgoing individual. Generally speaking, however, those people who are easily irritated or susceptible are considered difficult by everybody. If you are usually confronted with those types of people, you might recall trying hard not to upset them. You can't reason with an unreasonable person, but there are proven techniques to manage difficult conversations.

Always showing that you are listening to them is key to conducting a successful conversation. People are usually expressing anger as a consequence of frustration, as you might well know. Hence, that might be an indicator of feeling unheard and ignored. Treating people well and as you would like to be treated is always the first step to getting along with them. Moreover, if your interlocutor is showing signs of intolerance, don't ever be judgmental. Most of the time, if someone has this approach with you even before you start speaking, they are probably upset at something else. They might have an unpleasant situation at home or may be victims of injustice without you knowing about it. In the same way you have learned how to understand your own red flags, try to be understanding of other people's own issues. Verbal de-escalation tips include listening, staying calm, and looking for the individual's hidden needs.

What happens, however, when you are confronted with a person who is verbally attacking you? This might involve slightly more complex strategies to carry on a conversation. First, if you are a person prone to angry outbursts, you might know that seeing a person smiling when you are in the middle of an anger outburst is infuriating. The angry person might feel mocked and ridiculed. Another behavior to avoid is to constantly repeat "I understand," or "Stay calm," because the angry listener might interpret that as a sign of disregard. They might think that you are not listening to what they are saying and that you are putting no effort into understanding their point of view. As a result, they might get even angrier, and the conversation can turn into a fight. In similar circumstances, remember to keep a distance between yourself and your interlocutor. Try not to respond back with anger, and be compliant with the person. In this way, you are not submissive or obedient, as it might seem. On the contrary, you are showing maturity in recognizing the potential danger, and you are also contributing to other people's understanding of them being wrong. In fact, an angry individual is more likely to calm down if their debater does not respond with anger but with calm and firm behavior. Remember that one response does not fit all; you will need to remain agile when navigating illogical arguments or nonsensical responses. One of the most important aspects when speaking to an individual that does not care to listen, is knowing when to walk away. After employing all the seven Cs of communication and actively listening to the other party's point of view, you have done enough to respect the other person. If they are not willing to afford you that same courtesy and respect, it is all right to walk away from the situation to save yourself any wasted effort or potential escalation.

Expressing Yourself Without Anger

Being understanding of other people's anger, however, does not mean that you have to shut down your thoughts and opinions.

In this book, we have extensively talked about the importance of speaking up, expressing your feelings, and avoiding repressing your anger. At the same time, it is important that you master your communication skills and that you learn how to express your negative feelings without being aggressive.

To do that effectively, you first need to learn how to differentiate between an *argument* and a *fight*. The first is a conversation between two or more people who hold different opinions and discuss, through reasoning and logic, their respective points of view. A fight, on the other hand, is a discussion or very animated debate between people who are verbally or physically violent and who do not use any logical tool to defend their respective opinions. If you want to speak up in a productive way, you should ideally resort to the first option. Having a reasonable conversation avoids the listeners labeling you as "crazy" and makes them more likely to listen to you. Similarly, when addressing the other person, avoid labeling them based on their current behavior. During an argument, in fact, you should point out why the other person is upsetting you, rather than generalizing their momentary behavior as a part of their personality. Avoid calling them "stupid" or "crazy" and highlight why they are being unreasonable at that specific moment. This would show cooperation towards them, rather than making them feel like enemies.

Another good way to keep the conversation on good terms is to convey your emotions. Tell the other person how you are feeling at that moment, which would avoid giving the wrong impression of yourself. If you describe your emotions, the other person will not think of you as a know-it-all person and would be less likely to point fingers at you.

RESTORATIVE COMMUNICATION

You might find all these indications provided above useful when it comes to establishing new relationships with others or when you are occasionally confronted with other angry people. However, would that also work with your already consolidated relationships?

You might imagine that a radical and abrupt change in your relationship's quality is hard to achieve. So, in this regard, what would be the best approach to progressively bring your connection with your close ones to a better place?

Restorative communication is a group of techniques aimed at ameliorating relationships between individuals when harm and conflict have already occurred. This communication style is still based on the expression of feelings and mutual understanding, and it requires following some fundamental steps. The first step requires you to understand the nature of the conflict. Every verbal fight is based on the same universal structure: When you are angry at someone you always want to change their behavior until it gets closer to your interpretation of what is good and right. Second, you must become aware of what you usually *do* to change said behavior. The general tendency of people who want to change how other people act is by threatening them.

In your romantic relationship you might recall saying "If you don't change the way you behave, I will break up with you," or instead, you might have been told so. Restorative communication holds that relationships can be fixed by acquiring a solid verbal approach with your close ones; you should start feeling comfortable describing your needs and thoughts with your significant other or close ones because that is the only way to build relationships based on trust and mutual respect.

This approach has been extensively adopted by different institutions to reduce harm and restore relationships. In fact, restorative practice is a social science by itself, which studies and develops new techniques to ameliorate social bonds through decision-making and learning strategies. The International Institute for Restorative Practices (IIRP) has developed its own program to follow to repair social relationships (Wachtel, 2016). At that level, it is mostly designed to restore relationships for the general population security and to restore social order. This program aims at minimizing crime, reducing violent behavior, ameliorating social communication and connections between humans, and restoring relationships. This is because it has a general application: the premise that attempting to prevent conflict rather than punishing it can be applied to both institutional settings and everyday life. In fact, this program teaches everyone to have a preventive approach to relationships by adopting strategies that encourage a good living in society. In this way, relationships are turned into a learning opportunity, where every circumstance gives you the possibility to do better.

EMPOWER YOURSELF WITH SELF-EMPATHY

Exercise: My Empathy Level

This exercise is aimed at understanding how empathetic your approach to conversation usually is. In the following table, draw an *x* next to the affirmation that you deem true about your communication style in any given conversation. For the purpose of this exercise, try to think of a scenario where you and the interlocutor are having an argument and disagreeing over something.

During your conversation, you:

- Tell the person off; tell them they are wrong because they disagree with you.
- Carefully listen, be afraid of speaking over your interlocutor.
- Make fun of your interlocutor, take the chance to have a laugh.
- Ask your interlocutor for advice, but then feel weaker and compelled.
- Raise your voice and try to speak over your interlocutor.
- Give advice to your interlocutor but feel in a position of superiority.

- Look at the bright side of the situation and communicate it to your interlocutor.
- Carefully listen with the purpose of putting your interlocutor at ease.
- Jump to conclusions because you can't handle being told you are wrong.

Now that you have identified your behavior during a confrontational conversation, try to ask yourself why you engage in such behavior. If you have selected the third option, for example, you might be a sarcastic person, or you might hide the fear of measuring yourself with someone else.

The main premise of this exercise is to understand your communication style, which, most of the time, reflects your needs and past experiences. If your laugh is a coping mechanism to avoid confrontation, then being aware of it is the first step towards overcoming this limit of yours.

7

USE CBT STRATEGIES

The mind is everything. What you think, you become.

— BUDDHA

WHAT IS COGNITIVE BEHAVIORAL THERAPY?

Let us now shift our attention to one of the most famous and successful techniques to overcome psychological distress: cognitive behavioral therapy. In the last decade, this approach has gained a lot of scientific attention, with the attempt of minimizing the psychiatric use of medication and encouraging a more individually tailored psychological treatment. In fact, despite CBT becoming more and more standardized (following exact procedures and techniques based on different mental disorders), it also has the characteristic of being adaptable to everyone, considering all the complexities and singularities of each person. CBT has also risen from the need to not confine people inside boxes and labels but rather address each individual as such. Throughout the years, CBT has been used to treat a variety of conditions such as addictions, anxiety, and depressive disorders, as well as more debilitating mental illnesses, mostly gaining discrete success in clinical trials.

The main assumptions of this approach are the following. Most psychological distress can be treated by changing unhelpful ways of thinking, which arise from thinking patterns learned through experience. The first step towards changing patterns is recognizing the distorted stream of thought by doing "reality checks."

Usually, when this is carried out in therapy, the therapist helps the patient compare their opinions and beliefs (to identify underlying thinking patterns) with more useful and healthier thinking strategies, which should reflect reality. With CBT, patients learn new problem-solving skills and decision-making, as well as gain an overview of other people's general thinking, to better understand the behavior of others. Only after having identified the patients' thinking patterns (what they think, why they have a given opinion, what they think a consequence of action would be, etc.), the therapist would move forward into changing the "thinking wires" to address specific psychological issues.

CBT FOR ANGER MANAGEMENT

In CBT terms, anger management issues would arise when a person develops an insistent negative belief system, where every element of the person (emotions, values, opinions, etc.) are invested in negativity. Usually, in this scenario, every stream of the belief system influences the others; negative emotions lead to negative values, which in turn lead to negative opinions, and so on.

According to CBT, when a belief system is dysfunctional or flawed, it can be deconstructed and reconstructed in the best possible way. This is particularly useful for anger issues, and CBT has developed some core thinking strategies to treat them. If you are suffering from anger management issues and you label a person guilty for upsetting you, a CBT approach would focus on making you think that the person probably did not upset you intentionally and would give you a broader perspective on the event. It would also shift your attention to the stressor or trigger rather than on the person. The person upsetting you is just another human holding their own belief system which usually crashes with other people's. More specifically, because CBT holds that all behavioral patterns are learned because they are repeated, anger is regarded as an emotional response that can be changed with practice. There are several CBT techniques that can serve that purpose.

Enhanced Personal Awareness (EPA) is a CBT strategy that holds the belief that people are usually not aware of their anger triggers. Making them aware of them usually requires role-playing, where the therapist would try to trigger the patients in different ways until they would find the correct trigger. Other techniques to perform EPA are discussions with the therapist where they try to identify feelings and emotions triggered by given episodes and keeping a detailed day-to-day diary of changes in the thinking pattern.

Another famous CBT strategy is called Anger Disruption by Avoidance and Removal. Here the therapist would help you find ways that best work for you to momentarily remove yourself from the situation of anger. Still, through role-playing, your therapist might challenge you into reacting to your anger triggers in different ways from what you would normally do. For example, if your therapy journey has revealed that your most common reaction to anger is violence and confrontation, this exercise would then have you react in a withdrawal way: distracting yourself, engaging in other activities, or simply leaving the place could all be useful ways to modify your thinking and behavioral patterns.

Lastly, Attitude and Cognitive Change techniques focus on reframing given situations into more rational perspectives. If, while reconstructing a scenario, your therapist identifies an element that you see as particularly negative or catastrophic, they would work with you by changing the way you see that particular element.

CBT on Your Own

After having briefly mentioned how CBT can help deal with anger in therapy settings, let us now give a closer look at what can be done by ourselves, according to CBT theories.

The most important premise of this approach is the understanding that our behavior is the result of helpful/unhelpful thinking patterns, which can be changed by modifying those patterns. What is a typical pattern in which we all engage, but that causes significant mental distress? This is the frequent use of the "should/must" statements we impose on ourselves every day. According to cognitive behavior accounts, such statements are very much responsible for ruminative thoughts of panic, anxiety, and for anger disorders.

For instance, when you are facing a challenge and you try to deal with it by telling yourself, "I should not be affected by this," you automatically suppress all the detrimental feelings and bodily sensations that such a situation causes you. Suppressing something always means it will come back, and it will come back worse most of the time.

We tend to use should statements when we are engaging in a behavior that we don't want to accept, or of which we are particularly ashamed of. Think of the scenario where your daughter or son keeps on doing something that you find very upsetting. After arguing with them several times, you might opt for other solutions: you might start ignoring their behavior and simply tell yourself, "Stop getting upset about this, you should get over it." But, in reality, their behavior still causes you the same reaction, your body still reacts with anger, and your brain still registers their behavior as something very upsetting. You clearly have not solved the issue. Instead of "should" statements, you could try to rephrase your thought by expressing your real feelings: "This gets me very upset, and I wish it didn't," or, "I wish my son/daughter behaved in a different way." This totally different approach to the problem would make you feel less hopeless about change and would also help you process your real feelings.

Another activity you might want to engage in (considering both the journey of this book and the CBT approach) is a deep analysis of your negative thoughts related to anger. First, try to identify your thinking pattern. This includes investigating your thoughts-emotions-behaviors, as well as questioning what triggered them and what consequences they led to. Can you recall an upsetting event at your workplace? After having identified it, try to recall all the surrounding context. Thinking in a CBT approach, what were your initial thoughts at the time when your anger was triggered? How did that thought influence your immediate emotions? An example of this could be thinking of how rude your boss was to you and feeling extremely frustrated the second after.

And third, what behavior has this thought-emotion combo triggered in you? How did you react at that moment? After having reconstructed the whole scenario, you can now think of the purpose of your initial thought. By doing so, you might figure out that your negative thought had a protective purpose: It encouraged you to act against your rude boss. On the other hand, you could realize that your thought was influenced by your low mood that morning, which had you seeing everything in a dark light. Whatever realization you come up with, it would not have been possible if you didn't take the time to analyze your thought process. Without such analysis, you would have continued to feel the same anger without ever finding a resolution for it.

If you feel angry or upset without apparent reason, you might then be lamenting an unmet need. Feeling particularly angry in a disproportionate way as compared to the circumstance might be an alarm bell for something not quite good. If you are angry at work, you are probably being disrespected in some ways. If you are feeling angry at home, maybe your efforts are being disregarded. In this case, if you want to trace your negative thinking pattern, you might need to isolate the reason for your anger. Only after doing so, can you then proceed to develop new ways to meet your needs and expectations.

Now that you have identified your unmet need, you can proceed to act and ameliorate that specific situation. If you have realized that your boss is being disrespectful toward you, giving a reasonable voice to your anger might be a good solution. Try to employ the techniques of restorative conversations and make sure you address the problem without violence and rage. Remember that most of the time, the people who are hurting you are not even *aware* that they are doing so. Being diplomatic and rational is always a good solution.

EMPOWER YOURSELF WITH SELF-REFLECTION

Exercise: Thought Recorder

This exercise is aimed at having you practice the skill of analyzing your thought pattern. You will analyze in detail the thoughts that lead to your emotions in a given moment and the behavior that resulted from that

For this exercise, you might need a piece of paper and a pen where you can take your notes, by following the steps below.

1. Think of a time when you had an anger outburst and try to remember when it happened. This can be related to any sphere of your personal or working life. Take note of the day and time (approximately) when the event took place.

2. Write down a detailed description of the event you initially thought of. You should write it down in the first person singular so that you would feel more invested in the remembrance of the event. Also, try to describe the event chronologically so that you can analyze the event in a cause-consequence fashion.

3. Try to summarize in one word or phrase all the thoughts that came up in your mind at the time of that episode. What can you think of now that you have revived that negative circumstance in your life? The word or phrase that you will select to summarize all your ideas will now be labeled as an automatic or dysfunctional thought. A dysfunctional thought is a negatively biased perception about oneself, the world, and others. These thoughts make people feel powerless and hopeless and are usually the result of skewed interpretations of their surroundings.

> **a.** Very importantly, now that you are imagining that event so vividly, write down (next to the word describing the thought) the percentage of credibility. How much do you believe in the veracity of that thought? How true and real is it for you? Write down this score as a percentage.
>
> - An example of this could be summarizing the thought of the event into the phrase, "The worst afternoon of my week: 95%," and, "I am sure I will now run into other inconveniences: 80%." With this step, you express how much you were convinced that the negative

prediction of the event or day would have become true.

b. By using the same interval intensity scale, write down next to the main thought all the secondary emotions elicited and then write down the percentage of veracity next to them. What feelings did the dysfunctional thought elicit at the time? This will help you know, in the future, how you will be feeling shortly after having conceived a similar thought and perhaps help you divert the thought in time.

- An example of this could be feeling "frustrated: 90%," "disappointed: 100%," "in disagreement: 70%," and "hurt: 85%."

4. Then, it is the time to write down your cognitive distortions resulting from the thought, the event, and the emotions. Cognitive distortions are all the altered conclusions you jump to, following your automatic thought and the cognitive perception of the feeling of anger.

- If your dysfunctional thought was, "My son is lying to me," the event that followed was, "I told him about my concerns in a violent manner which led to a bad fight," and the main emotion was "frustration." The cognitive distortions could have been, "My son does not respect me as a mother and woman, he does not appreciate me."

5. Now that you have all the elements of the event in your hands, it is time to replace a piece. You can now rethink your automatic and dysfunctional thoughts to find a more positive solution. This is very important because it sets the foundation of your future behavior. If your automatic thought is dysfunctional, you will most likely cause a fight. If, on the other hand, you manage to conceive a positive thought from the beginning, you will then resolve the situation amicably.

6. Having turned the tables, can you now think of different possible outcomes for the event? Write down your new perception percentage, the degree of veracity of your initial dysfunctional thought.

Ideally, you have acquired a broader perspective as well as an external one of the events. You will now be able to portray different outcomes and feel less strongly about the initial automatic thought.

The results might not be so immediate, but if this exercise is repeated in the long-term, it can help you modify your thought pattern into a more positive one.

CONCLUSION

If you reached this point in the book, you should be proud of yourself! You have certainly started a journey towards better management of your anger issues and an understanding of the principal mechanisms underlying anger outbursts.

In the first chapter, we looked at the preliminary elements to understand the concept of anger itself. Through a physiological and evolutionary account, we discussed how the roots of anger in humans emerged and discovered that this emotion is a survival tool to help individuals face adversities. It is an ally of fear, but while fear acts when the danger is only perceived, anger helps react when no other escape is left. It is an important tool that we have inherited from our ancestors, and, for this reason, we don't have to erase it from our personality but only learn how to manage it.

We as humans have mostly inherited features throughout evolution that serve a specific purpose today. So, what purpose can anger serve us in the current society? As humans, and especially as women, we have many reasons to exhibit anger and frustration nowadays. We have talked about social injustices and the extreme pressure we are under, which constantly endangers our mental health.

Despite all the latest advances in gender rights, the configuration of our society still implicitly and explicitly imposes expected behaviors on women. The "act like a lady" commandment is still very much a reality, and certainly has consequences on what we feel and think. In both formal (workplaces, relationships with strangers) and informal (family and friends) environments, we are always expected to exhibit a certain behavior. People don't expect us to speak up and use our voices to fight for our rights, have arguments with authoritarian figures, be too extroverted, and have outstanding leadership skills.

Considering this analysis demonstrates how anger can warn us of situations of injustice, we have moved towards an understanding of this feeling. We have figured out that, at the base of anger, there are always precipitating events—triggers. We now can understand what a trigger is, how to identify it, and how to shift its purpose. We want our triggers to be our allies: They must be indicators of injustice and encourage us to look for a change. We certainly don't want them to be elements in the environment that cause unmanageable anger outbursts and make us change personalities in a detrimental manner. Understanding our triggers is key to managing our rage.

The following take-home message was that, if anger is triggered by something present in the external environment, there is always a root cause. In this way, we have learned to dig into our past and get a grip on our hidden weaknesses. Some of us might have dealt with particularly complex trauma in the past, and others might have had unresolved issues from a young age. In case you find difficulties tracing back your trauma, it is always a good idea to turn to a professional figure who could certainly shed light on your past.

There are avenues you can take to look after yourself on a daily basis and strengthen the lessons learned throughout this book. The importance of self-care and a good dose of mindfulness and meditation always helps. We have seen that mindfulness works as a cushion for anger, such that it would equip you with resistance and patience. If practiced correctly, it can even make you less sensitive to anger cues and, overall, a calmer person. If you liked how mindfulness exercises calmed you down and wanted to acquire a broader grasp on psychological techniques, then you probably enjoyed the CBT chapter. Cognitive Behavioral Therapy gives you a cause-consequence perspective, making you understand that certain thoughts lead to certain emotions and trigger certain behaviors. Changing specific pieces of your mental puzzles can eventually help you to change your behavior and make you a more aware individual.

Finally, we discussed the power of communication. You have interactions with people every day, and it is fundamental for you to know how to manage them in the best possible way. After having practiced your constructive conversation skills, you might now have a better understanding of how to confront different types of people and how to avoid violent encounters. Furthermore, after reading the restorative communication part, you might now have mastered new techniques to resolve past or existing conflicts with your significant other or your close ones.

The Story of Jessica, A Mother

Jessica is a 35-year-old charming and charismatic woman who has a 6-year-old daughter. She contacted a therapist to help her deal with her highly irrational anger outbursts. In fact, Jessica reported having severe rage attacks whenever her daughter would do things that generally all children do. These would include taking her time before choosing the color of her clothes, taking time to get ready in the morning, or leaving clothes lying around in the house. Jessica would then get suddenly very upset, and she would leave the room to go punch a pillow. Such anger outbursts were having a detrimental effect on Jessica's relationship with her daughter, as well as making the little girl very afraid of her own mother. For this reason, Jessica started to go to therapy following sessions of emotional regulations with a therapist, which eventually made her anger outbursts stop. After each session, she would make an appointment for a follow-up meeting weeks later to make sure that the anger issues did not come back. Jessica was extremely relieved that she managed to fix this impactful issue in her life, and she is now having her best time with her little daughter.

Jessica's story shows how even the most illogical and irrational anger issues can be solved if one takes the time to look inside oneself.

Your Chance to Change

Regardless of your advances in your anger management skills, you should always keep in mind that human nature is complex and scattered. We are constantly experiencing ungraspable emotions, which is what ultimately makes us so interesting and fascinating. In light of this, you should always love yourself and look at the inner you with comprehension and tenderness. You should also keep in mind that the journey toward a better self might be long and tortuous, and that perseverance and reliance will be your best friends.

This book is here to remind you that countless women have gone through anger management issues, some of whom experienced traumatic events in their pasts (think of Laurie Christopher's story). Yet each one of them finds the strength and the tools to challenge their anger issues to become the best version of themselves.

And you, are you ready to become that woman?

You are now familiar with many different tools to address your issues. However, always remember to ask for professional assistance from psychologists or mental health workers when things get unmanageable; support figures are always out there to come and help you when you most need it. Comorbidities with other conditions, such as depression or anxiety, are, most of the time, very hard to detect and certainly require a professional perspective. However, when looking at the brightest side of things, the resolution of your anger issues is inside of you, and you only need to master the techniques to find them.

LEAVE A REVIEW

If you have enjoyed reading this book and completing the exercises provided, kindly leave a review. Just scan the QR code below!

Hopefully, with your encouraging words, women going through the same struggles will be encouraged to undertake the same anger management and self-empowerment journey.

A PLACE TO GROW

In times of great stress or adversity, it's always best to keep busy, to plow your anger and your energy into something positive.

— LEE IACOCCA

This section of the book is specifically tailored for you to continue your anger management journey by yourself. It will be made of a blank template to enable you to apply your learnings in the future, and it will also be always available to you anytime that you need a moment of self-reflection.

To a person that has not gone through the whole book, these questions might seem uninspired and pointless. However, to anyone who has reached this point going through every step of this book, these questions will bring you back to all the explanations provided above by refreshing your memory and giving you another chance to challenge yourself.

1. When did the event happen? Try to write down an approximate date and time of the event you are thinking about.
2. What happened? Write a detailed description of the event. Include a description of the place you were at the time of the event, who were you with, and who you confronted.
3. What were your thoughts? What were your feelings? Now try to describe anything related to your emotional state at that point, including bodily sensations.
4. How angry did you feel? Write down a number to indicate a score on your anger scale.
5. How did you react to the event? Describe your immediate actions and the actions of the other person
6. What were the consequences of your actions? Describe the effects that your actions had on reality.

7. How did you feel after the event in relation to your actions? Did you feel guilty? Sad? Write down your feelings.
8. Now, picture again the initial event and think of other possible thoughts you could have had. Which thoughts can you think of?
9. What consequences would these new thoughts have had on the event?
10. What emotions would you have felt if things went differently? How would a change in your thinking have changed the outcomes of the situation?

JUST FOR YOU!

A FREE GIFT for our readers!
This Rapid Relaxation Guide is a popular CBT treatment to relax, relieve stress and tension, anywhere at any time,
in **seconds**! Scan the QR code below!

REFERENCES

Abu Alwafa, R., Badrasawi, M., & Haj Hamad, R. (2021). Prevalence of premenstrual syndrome and its association with psychosocial and lifestyle variables: A cross-sectional study from Palestine. *BMC Women's Health, 21*(1). https://doi.org/10.1186/s12905-021-01374-6

Allan, A. J. (2009). The importance of being a "lady": Hyper-femininity and heterosexuality in the private, single-sex primary school. *Gender and Education, 21*(2), 145–158. https://doi.org/10.1080/09540250802213172

Blair, R. J. R. (2011). Considering anger from a cognitive neuroscience perspective. *Wiley Interdisciplinary*

Reviews: Cognitive Science, *3*(1), 65–74. https://doi.org/10.1002/wcs.154

Buddle, M. (2006). "You have to think like a man and act like a lady": Businesswomen in British Columbia, 1920-80. *BC Studies: The British Columbian Quarterly*, (151), 69-95.

Campbell, A. (2004). Female competition: Causes, constraints, content, and contexts. *Journal of Sex Research*, *41*(1), 16–26. https://doi.org/10.1080/00224490409552210

Catalyst. (2018). *Quick Take: Women in science, technology, engineering, and mathematics (STEM) - Catalyst*. Catalyst. https://www.catalyst.org/research/women-in-science-technology-engineering-and-mathematics-stem/

Chatterjee, R. (2020). *As menopause nears, be aware it can trigger depression and anxiety, too*. NPR.org. https://www.npr.org/sections/health-shots/2020/01/16/796682276/for-some-women-nearing-menopause-depression-and-anxiety-can-spike

Chemaly, S. (2019, August 28). *Why women don't get to be angry*. Medium. https://gen.medium.com/rage-becomes-her-why-women-dont-get-to-be-angry-b2496e9d679d

Cirino, E. (2018, December 3). *Anger management exercises: 9 exercises to help curb your anger.* Healthline. https://www.healthline.com/health/anger-management-exercises

Cowen, A. S., & Keltner, D. (2017). Self-report captures 27 distinct categories of emotion bridged by continuous gradients. *Proceedings of the National Academy of Sciences*, 114(38), E7900–E7909. https://doi.org/10.1073/pnas.1702247114

Deschênes, S. S., Dugas, M. J., Fracalanza, K., & Koerner, N. (2012). The role of anger in generalized anxiety disorder. *Cognitive Behaviour Therapy*, 41(3), 261–271. https://doi.org/10.1080/16506073.2012.666564

Funk, C., & Parker, K. (2018). *For media or other inquiries: "Women and men in stem often at odds over workplace equity."* https://vtechworks.lib.vt.edu/bitstream/handle/10919/92671/WomenSTEEMWorkplace.pdf?sequence=1

Fottrell, Q. (2019, November 29). *"Women are judged for*

being emotional" —Yet it's more acceptable for men to get upset and angry, female executives say. MarketWatch. https://www.marketwatch.com/story/serena-williams-got-angry-at-the-us-open-final-and-paid-a-heavy-priceworking-women-say-this-sounds-eerily-familiar-2018-09-10

Greenfieldboyce, N. (2019). If you're often angry or irritable, you may be depressed. *NPR.org.* https://www.npr.org/sections/health-shots/2019/02/04/689747637/if-youre-often-angry-or-irritable-you-may-be-depressed?t=1652661399172

Judd, L. L., Schettler, P. J., Coryell, W., Akiskal, H. S., & Fiedorowicz, J. G. (2013). Overt irritability/anger in unipolar major depressive episodes. *JAMA Psychiatry, 70*(11), 1171. https://doi.org/10.1001/jamapsychiatry.2013.1957

Lois, E. (2016, December 27). *Act like a lady: 5 etiquette rules that still apply today.* Career Girl Daily. https://www.careergirldaily.com/act-like-a-lady-5-etiquette-rules-that-still-apply-today/

Kashdan, T. B., Goodman, F. R., Mallard, T. T., & DeWall, C. N. (2015). What triggers anger in everyday life? Links to the intensity, control, and regulation of these emotions, and personality traits. *Journal of Personality*, *84*(6), 737–749. https://doi.org/10.1111/jopy.12214

Kubzansky, L. D., Sparrow, D., Jackson, B., Cohen, S., Weiss, S. T., & Wright, R. J. (2006). Angry breathing: A prospective study of hostility and lung function in the Normative Aging Study. *Thorax*, *61*(10), 863–868. https://doi.org/10.1136/thx.2005.050971

Litvak, P. M., Lerner, J. S., Tiedens, L. Z., & Shonk, K. (2010). "Fuel In The Fire: How Anger Impacts Judgment and Decision-Making." In *International handbook of anger: Constituent and concomitant biological, psychological, and social processes*. Springer.

Vassar, G. (2011a). *Do you know your anger triggers?* Lakeside. https://lakesidelink.com/blog/lakeside/do-you-know-your-anger-triggers/

McDonald, P. (2012). Workplace sexual harassment 30 years on: A review of the literature. *International Journal of Management Reviews*, *14*(1), 1–17. https://doi.org/10.1111/j.1468-2370.2011.00300.x

Mostofsky, E., Penner, E. A., & Mittleman, M. A. (2014). Outbursts of anger as a trigger of acute cardiovascular events: A systematic review and meta-analysis. *European Heart Journal*, *35*(21), 1404–1410. https://doi.org/10.1093/eurheartj/ehu033

Novaco, R. W. (2011). Anger dysregulation: Driver of violent offending. *Journal of Forensic Psychiatry & Psychology*, *22*(5), 650–668. https://doi.org/10.1080/14789949.2011.617536

Premenstrual dysphoric disorder: Symptoms & treatment. (2020). Cleveland Clinic. https://my.clevelandclinic.org/health/articles/9132-premenstrual-dysphoric-disorder-pmdd#:~:text=Premenstrual%20dysphoric%20disorder%20(PMDD)%20is

Romero-Martínez, A., Lila, M., Vitoria-Estruch, S., & Moya-Albiol, L. (2014). High immunoglobulin A levels mediate the association between high anger expression and low somatic symptoms in intimate partner violence perpetrators. *Journal of Interpersonal Violence*, *31*(4), 732–742. https://doi.org/10.1177/0886260514556107

Thomas, S. P. (2005). Women's anger, aggression, and violence. *Health Care for Women International*, *26*(6), 504–522. https://doi.org/10.1080/07399330590962636

Wachtel, T. (2016). A restorative practices perspective: governance and authority. *MINORIGIUSTIZIA, 1*, 49–56. https://doi.org/10.3280/mg2016-001006

Williams, C. (2018, September 11). *Why aren't women allowed to be angry?* Electric Literature. https://electricliterature.com/why-arent-women-allowed-to-be-angry/

이동민. (2019, February 8). *Majority of working women quit during first pregnancy.* Yonhap News Agency. https://en.yna.co.kr/view/AEN20190208003100320

Printed in Great Britain
by Amazon